I0153464

Discovering Your True Worth:

Awakening to New Possibilities

By Rev. Dr. Gordon Van Namee

Discovering Your True Worth:

Awakening to New Possibilities

© Copyright, 2014

By

Gordon Van Namee

ISBN-978-0-9852206-7-9

Library of Congress-in-Publication Data

Cover designed by Sally Rice

Photography

DGPUBLISHING, INC. 2720 Blair Stone Rd.
Tallahassee, FL 32304
www.dgpublishingpress.com
850-878-0003

Acknowledgement

Above all I want to acknowledge the reality of the Lord who inspires me and guides me in real time and in a state of present love. This is the reality that He has awakened me to (Ephesians 5:14). Above all this is the most intimate, practical and meaningful relationship in my life. I also want to thank those who have helped me along the way, from editing to publishing and throughout the marketing process. When community becomes an extension of the initial relationship with Christ Jesus then amazing strength and benefits are realized. As I have written this book, I realize that in the pronoun I, there exists the reality of a complete community. Only God through Christ Jesus could create this effort and open my heart to those who share the healing message of this writing. In this, my thankful blessings go out to all along the way that have been such a blessing to me.

TABLE OF CONTENTS

Forward

It would be presumptuous for me to say that this writing will change the way that human nature is understood. That is, it would be presumptuous if I were putting forth this position on my own – however that is not the case, it is God and the very Spirit of God through the Word that proclaims this eternal truth! I am simply bringing this truth to focus. It is the reality upon which all individuals can be healed, enhanced and encouraged. It is the radical truth that should be used in all realistic personal counseling and personal therapy. Once a person realizes the significance of this shift in the reality of the inner-being of humankind, then and only then will true human healing come about. Any other psychological approach will fall short and be wasteful. Not only is this the pivot point for the healing and growth of the individual but it is the hope for the human culture as a whole, without which there will always be systematic dysfunction in the individual and society. The transformation of the individual must be based in truth and by reimaging the individual in this truth, the culture as a whole has the opportunity to be reimaged. May it begin with you – the reader!

Introduction

I have found that most people, to a large extent, are a product of their environment and that often, if not always, leaves them wounded and hurt. It leaves them in a state of *lack of fulfillment* and not in a place of reaching their full potential and true happiness. What is the center of the source of your worth, the source that you go to in need of strength as you face the challenges of the world? Do you truly know the source of your strength? When crisis sets in where do you turn?

It is my contention that where we find the source of our worth will be the source of our strength and that will determine our success or failure in life. It is the well that we draw from as we go through life's decisions, challenges and struggles. If we are misguided by our own lack of understanding as to what we truly are as individuals then that will cause us to have *diminished potential* and often lead to *failure or lack of joy.* The accumulated understanding of who we are as persons - our sense of worth, is mostly a product of what others think. That forms what is known as one's self-worth. I will show that self-worth is a false and harmful concept. I will show that one's true worth and only valid worth is *God-*

worth. I will take you on a journey of recon-struction in reestablishing your true under-standing of your worth and this will ultimately lead you to *fuller possibilities in life and a far greater degree of happiness.*

You are the most precious sight that God knows; that's right you are a *delight* to God's heart.[1] Yet, in our world we are often told that we are not worthy, that we are useless, insufficient, defective, just not what we need to be and lacking in some or all manner of being. Here, we can see that there are two different forces at work, one which creates, lifts up and enhances – God, and one that tears down, demeans and destroys – the force of the world.

As you have most likely experienced this reality, so have I, and I want to take you on a journey – *to rediscover the real you*, the truth of your real worth. The reality is that most people who are hurt by this deception of insufficiency don't really understand the truth of what is hurting them and they often can't see the richness of who they really are because of the lie that they have been told and they have accepted. The reality of this deception is not subject to be found in any one aspect of society, yet it is more prevalent in some

---

[1] Isaiah 62:4.

aspects than others. It can be found in those who profess love, even Christian love or in the most ungodly. It seems to be an equal-opportunity destroyer of character and one's true value.

As I write this it is a message for all of God's children. Yet, it is written through the reality of Jesus Christ for Christians and non-Christians. There is one truth for one's source of individual worth and it is a need for all of humanity. Anything else, by its own nature is self-destructive. Jesus has told us, "You shall know the truth and the truth shall make you free."[2] It is within this discovery of truth that you will be awakened to your true reality of worth and in fact to the only basis for your factual worth. It will bring riches into your heart and soul beyond any measure that you have realized to this point. This will be a life-saving discovery – NO MATTER WHO YOU ARE! You may say, "I know who I am," well, my friend, you may have an idea but as you read this understanding you will discover there is a whole lot more to you than you have ever imagined. It is my goal to guide you through this refocusing process and allow you to discover the fullness of your worth – it will open your eyes to riches beyond what you now know, as Jesus tells us, "At that day you will know that I am

---

[2] John 8:32

in My Father and you in Me and I in you."[3] Today is the day that you can discover this reality and your true *God-worth*.

The one thing I ask is that you come to this writing with an open mind and a prayerful heart. Read to seek the truth and as Jesus has told us, that shall make you free. We as humans are bound by the substance of our environment and that is often what produces our sense of worth. Bound is the key word here, our environment and culture binds each of us with various levels of lies, dysfunction and stunted growth, perpetuating these lies within each individual passing from one generation to another. When one is bound they are restricted from growth.

If you have ever planted a tree or plant from a nursery one of the first things you do is to take it out of the original pot to place it in the ground. Before you place that bulb of root structure into the new ground there is one very important thing that you must do, you must break apart the root structure of the bulb. As it is in the pot its roots are inter-tangled and restricted from growth. The root structure of the bulb takes the shape of the pot and is inward grown. See, if you don't break those roots loose they will still think

---

[3] John 14:20.

that they are bound within the limits of that original pot and will not grow to full potential. The plant will be deceived and think it is still in that original pot. The plant will struggle, often fail or have its growth stunted. By breaking the roots loose, gently with one's fingers, the unbound roots will reach down into that new earth, its new environment and find greater nutrition and exponential growth. Each of us who is willing to follow this journey to seek truth in ourselves will discover this new place of strength, creative power and personal reimaging – it will be a loosening of what binds us and we will be set free. When Jesus called Lazarus out of the grave, who had been dead for four days, Lazarus was bound with grave cloths around his body and face which would have restricted any vision or movement, Jesus said to them, "Loose him and let him go."[4] The first thing that Lazarus saw as they took off the grave cloths from his face was Jesus in all of His glory and grace. Lazarus' life was never the same. It is realistic to say that Lazarus got a new understanding of life, new strength, a new footing in reality and was able to lose all fear. It is also safe to say that Lazarus developed a completely new sense of personal worth as a result of this revealing event. What a

---

[4] John 11:44.

transformation! Certainly from that point on no one could tell Lazarus that he was lacking in worth- he had been given true worth and esteem which could not be shaken. *He had been transformed into the living awareness of his worth being grounded in Jesus Christ and Him only* – not of the world since he left that awareness in the tomb of the dead. All the negativity received from others, the anger, aggression, hostility and proclaimed worthlessness was no longer part of Lazarus' life for he died to this world and arose in the glory of Jesus. From this point forward it is Jesus and Jesus alone who Lazarus would reflect upon to know his true worth – he realized the truth that Jesus and Jesus alone has true authority over life, everything else is reflective of that fact and anything else is superficial.

How will this happen you ask, how can something so profound be possible? Well, it is possible because it is of God and not my doing. I will help you to *"see through the eyes of heaven"* which is the only true way to know your true worth and to discover your riches in this place. What I offer you, is a *recalibration* of your reality that I am sure will lift you up to new heights. Even if you are saying to yourself, "I'm ok." I believe that you will discover in this reading that you too have been deceived by a negative and dysfunctional culture. The reality is that we as humans live in a broken and dysfunctional world and it has its fallout and that fallout radiates to all throughout society. Counter to this dysfunctional and destructive force is a greater force that is healing and life renewing in all ways. *Like Lazarus, you can share the glory of Jesus with you in this place and reach Godly potential.* That is my promise to you – this writing offers you, no matter what point you are at on your life journey the opportunity to renew the reality of your worth and thus, gain amazing new insight and purpose.

1

The Truth Concerning Self-Worth

Let no corrupt word proceed out of your mouth,
But what is good for necessary edification,
That it may impart grace to the hearers.[5]

There I was, sitting in the office of the guidance counselor. It was a dreaded place for any high school student. It was my turn. I wasn't sure how to feel, whether or not to be nervous. He had always been nice to me but I knew very well I was under his authority and was hoping for the best. All the teachings, books, years of learning and facts upon facts stored in my head, but it all comes down to people and relationships and how we treat each other along the way. The question was, how would I be treated this day?

What made this day so special was that it was my day to come before the guidance counselor and receive his appraisal of my status as a student,

---

[5] Ephesians 4:29.

a person and my future potential. Truly, I wasn't quite sure of what to expect from the whole thing. The other students told me it was no big deal and that's about all they said. There I sat, a tall, thin, young kid. He was in his traditional suit and tie seated behind his desk, as he welcomed me. I politely and meekly took my place in the chair facing him. How vulnerable I felt, as if he held my future in his hands. What was he about to say?

I was a typical high school student. I enjoyed life more than I did books and my grades reflected that decision of priorities. It was my senior year. I was hopeful about life and yet the idea of entering the big world outside of those halls which had insulated me for the past twelve years caused no little amount of fear in my inner being. On the surface I appeared confident and happy but within there was a sense of insufficiency. I wonder if you know what I mean, have you ever felt less than worthy or inadequate? The irony is that I didn't even understand how vulnerable I was as I prepared to go out into life on my own.

"Well, Gordon" he started out, "you've always been a pleasant student to have around. You have never caused any real problems and most people like you. But your grades, well, they are not good. You won't be able to get into college with these grades and I don't know what you are going to do with your life – it isn't going to be easy. You are just managing to graduate and frankly if I were you I would go out and find the first factory job you can find and keep it. It's about all you are capable of so be happy with it." I sat there in silence listening to this verdict. At that moment I felt the foolishness of my years of having a good time and my lack of study, but I knew I could be something if I applied myself, yet he just told me I am a complete failure, a nobody, without hope. I was stunned and left shattered in pieces. It wouldn't seem possible, but I left even more meek and feeling less worthy than when I walked into his office. He had a position, he was accomplished and had security, I was left with nothing.

The one thing I did have was a relationship with a girl that I had been dating for almost a year. Our love for each other was great. She believed in me and may have been the one reason that I didn't go into a state of despair or even worse, a state of depression. I did believe in myself, but if nobody believed in me maybe they were right and I was wrong – well, that could have been my logic if it hadn't been for this girl in my life who later became my wife.

My self-worth was at an all time low. That guidance counselor took what little I had left of feeling good about myself and ground it into dust. Ironically, at the end of the conversation he was feeling fine about himself. That is what happens with *worth-destructive* people. They leave a wake of broken hearts, hopes and images in their path. It is a cultural cancer of the soul perpetuated from one's own misunderstanding of self-image.

It took me years to get beyond that man's condemning words; his lack of having faith in possibilities and his lack of hope in hope itself. Who was he that he had the right and authority to pronounce me as good as dead? Have you ever had such negative words said about you in any way which made you feel less than human? Have you ever felt the words of destruction reach into your heart and take away your hope for life? That's where I was, my spirit was so low in my thin six foot figure of a young man. If only people could have seen the real me they would have seen only a shadow in place of my human structure.

Many years have come and gone since then and I have achieved many victories and fulfilled many possibilities far beyond my early dreams but that experience has left me with a resounding reality and that is this - *self-worth is a false concept.* Self-worth is built upon what a person receives from their environment, from the voices that they hear throughout their years, from their beginning before they can walk to the times of facing their challenges. It's these voices that shape you and try to form who you are and who you think you can become. They often speak out of their own shortcomings, pain, disappointments and failures. The voices that say you are too short, too tall, too dark, too light, too pretty, too ugly, too dull, too common, too fat, too thin and the words that you are just plain not good enough are all registered into a bundle of self which becomes the image of one's worth formed by the world. These are the voices that like tapes play over and over in one's mind, you know them, you hear them, and they do not mean good for you. You cannot reach a state of peace with these words of negativity repeating themselves within you – *you must seek a higher level of consciousness.* In a world that is so negative, hurtful and broken, does it make sense to let that voice determine who you are and who you will be? *Self-worth is dictated by the world and creates humans out of its own insufficiency.* It is the perpetuating wave of dysfunction flowing throughout the generations. *There are those who break the cycle but it is only by recalibrating one's source of worth – finding the only source of one's true worth in a place of real love.* At that time I did not know Jesus, I only knew those destructive words spoken by a worldly man who himself had certainly limited his own potential by limiting others. He was not an encourager but a discourager. He thought he was being realistic but that is only because he was based upon the hopeless reality of a human-centered culture, which is a culture of sub-achievement, of limitations and insufficiency. My awareness of a relationship with Jesus would come years later, how much pain I could have avoided in my life if someone would have offered me the truth about my source of worth; if I had only met someone who understood the principle that I want to share with you. This is one reason that I feel so passionate about this truth and this reality. I have lived with the pain, suffering and failure of other's own dysfunction projected upon myself and it caused me great harm, but it did not need to be that way and it doesn't need to be that way in your life.

I want to offer to you, to suggest, that you are very special and wonderfully made and that you have potential beyond the limits of your own self-imagination.[6] I want to sit down with you, not as that guidance counselor sat with me in his limited and negative mindset, but in a spirit of truth and tell you that if you are relying upon self-worth you will fall far short of your true worth and God's ability to fill you with happiness. Sol Stein, in one of his books, tells of an author by the name of Christy Brown "who had the use of his brain, the little toe on his left foot, and little else."[7] Yet, he became a famous author, overcoming all probabilities and impossibilities. I have to wonder how many times people looked at him and said,

---

[6] Psalm 139:14.
[7] Sol Stein, *Stein on Writing* (New York: St. Martin's Press, 1995), 12.

"Oh, how sad – you can't do anything!" People can be cruel you know, don't you? Think for a moment about all of the negative words that might have been spoken to him through his young years. Even before he could talk certainly people would lament with his mother out loud in front of him and say their little phrases of despair. This child was so deformed that any worldly minded person would certainly reject the possibility of success for his future. It was his mother who never gave up on him and was the voice of an angel who encouraged him to see what others could not see. The Bible tells us that God has created each of us in the image of perfect truth and love and that God has a specific purpose for each of us. *One of the main teachings of the Bible is that when one finds true awareness of a living relationship with Jesus Christ then and only then does the potential of the person excel beyond any measure of their imagination.*[8] What I want to say to you as I talk to you is that you have *God-worth within you* and that if you will rely upon your God-worth and set aside your self-worth you will find your true being and the wonder of your true potential. This is your true

---

[8] Philippians 1:6 & Ephesians 3:19-20.

worth and this is the journey I want to introduce you to and release you into. Just like Lazarus coming out of the tomb to realize his renewed centering upon Jesus, I want you to find that new reality that will give you a fresh new start and a new focus for your real being. Lazarus left what was of his old self in the tomb. When he was unbound from the grave cloths he came into a new awareness of the shared glory of Jesus – his sense of worth was radically changed. He realized that it was Jesus and Jesus alone who had authority over who he was as a person and he realized that he was filled with the power of Christ within him. In the writing of the Letter to the Philippians Apostle Paul says, "I can do all things through Christ who strengthens me."[9] Do you know this power of God-worth within you? Do you have that truth within you or are you living in the limitation of the world's negativity – in a state of self-worth?

Self-worth brings each of us under its own power and that source of power is subject to the

---

[9] Philippians 4:13.

ebbs and flows of the world. It causes a person to be part of the *self-collapse syndrome* that rides the waves of Wall Street as it goes from boom to bust, or fantasies of emotions that go from happiness to depression and back again, or the self that is built upon the words of a loved one who from time to time speaks hurt and pain into you instead of words of life and growth. There is a path to true joy and full potential and that is to discover that one's true worth is centered upon the presence of God within – it is called *God-worth*. This is the true meaning of your worth. It is a path to a life of *stability* and *certainty*. It is a path of understanding how truly special you are and seeing the amazing potential you have within you. *It is built upon eternal truth and perfect love and not the winds of society.* What you will gain is the potential of your true esteem, not self-esteem but *God-esteem*. Just like the author and writer, Christy Brown, you will have the potential to go beyond any measure of what others say you are capable of accomplishing. Come and join me in this conversation and discover the blessedness of your true being.

Jesus Wants You to Hear the Truth:
Jesus is that right and good voice to uplift us and

tells us He will speak into our hearts of "what is good for necessary edification, that it may impart grace to the hearers." Jesus wants you to find this truth that you will be built up, reimaged in the reality of His unbounded love and encouraged for your life's journey. Those who speak words of corruption will no longer have power over you. You will be sent free from what binds you. See Exodus 3:1-10.

A Moment of Reflection:

Consider your life. Are you where God wants you to be or have you limited your goals, your potential because of what others have said to you? Even if you are achieving cultural success are you feeling fulfilled and at peace in your inner heart? Do you ever have doubts about your worth or value as a person? Please stop here and pause, contemplate what I am asking you and be honest with yourself.

Intentional Action:

Certainly you have seen a beautiful sunrise at some point in your life. Think about that sunrise, picture it in your mind for a moment and then think about the source of light that makes for the brilliance of that sunrise with all of its potential.

That source doesn't change, but is affected by the weather on earth, from clouds to smog. The source of light remains the same in all of its potential and power. However, each day it may not be seen or only partially seen – yet it is still there as bright as ever. Coming to the reality of God-esteem allows you to realize that brightness no matter what type of day it is. Jesus says, "I am the light of the world. Whoever follows Me will not walk in darkness but have the light of life."[10] Take a moment to consider what your life would be like if you could see the light of that sunrise within your heart and soul at all times even when there is struggle in your life. What would happen if that became your only source of truth? What would you do with your personal clouds of being misrepresented by others? Would you want them to block that light? How could that light change your attitude towards yourself and your place in the world?

Write Some of Your Thoughts:

I want to encourage you to write some of your thoughts, what you are feeling, what you feel about your personal worth or maybe the things

---

[10] John 8:12.

that have formed your worth or reflect upon what you have just read and what it might mean for your life. (As you do this it will act as a journal for you to integrate what you are learning. It will record your feelings and help to move you forward in your growth towards a stronger and more authentic you.)

_____
_____
_____
_____
_____
_____
_____
_____
_____
_____
_____

2

A New Beginning

Therefore, if anyone is in Christ, he or she is a new creation; old things have passed away; behold, all things have become new. [11]

The words that are spoken to us from our youngest time can sometimes be hurtful and even painful. What causes the hurt and pain is that we take ownership of those words. Another way of saying this is that we accept these words as truth into our being. These false images become our reflection of self that we look at in our minds day in and day out and this causes us to feel unworthy and insufficient. If you have ever come to a challenge and felt defeated before you begin then you know what I am saying to you. *Self-doubt is a prime result of carrying the false-baggage of self-worth.* Think about your own life, are you positive or negative when it comes to the assessment that you have of yourself?

Let me be very clear here, no one person can do everything. It is good to have a realistic view

---

[11] 2 Corinthians 5:17.

of what we can do and what we cannot do. Each of us is given gifts and skills by our creator. Yet there is a difference of believing in God for what we can do and having self-worth. Once we shift to believing in God for what we can do we will be given all that we need by God for what He calls us to do. Once you make the shift from looking to your own limited strength to leaning upon the God-strength within you, you will lose self-doubt.

To start the process of coming into the fullness of your true humanity you must first do some house cleaning – get rid of some of the old baggage that is weighing you down. Once you start to clear out some of this old stuff space will be created for something new. In this way you will start to take authority over your life and take authority over the false pictures that others have projected upon you. As you move the old stuff out I want you to replace it with the things about you that are true which is the *fertile ground* for you to reach your full potential. Remember this is a process - your hurt, pain and false concept was built over a period of years and its renewal, reimaging, and rebuilding will take time and effort. What is most amazing is that Jesus upon the cross shows that He is able to overcome all of the negativity of this world, the sin and false teachings, and to rise again in victory and glory to be the one to help you!

You must first anchor yourself in truth, the truth that will lead you to recovery from being on a series of life support systems that will eventually fail. These life support systems are built upon a fallen and deceiving world, going from one broken feeling of self-worth to another. Have you at times ever felt like a ping-pong ball being bounced around by others that you interact with? You must come to a truth that has the power to change your attitude towards yourself into the true God-worth that you are. Apostle Paul, from the first century, in his letter to the Romans, says this, "If God is for us, who can be against us?"[12] I want you to think about this. He says these words towards the very end of his ministry, a ministry in which the forces of the

world came upon him with hatred, pain and violence. He says that, from the Jews (his own people,) five times he received forty stripes minus one. These lashes to the flesh were so severe that each time it would leave him near death. The pain of each lashing is beyond measure. Three times he was beaten with rods. Once he was stoned, which means that he was given up to a formal means of

---

[12] Romans 8:31.

execution, most likely physically broken and disfigured for life from this misguided action of self-righteous people who lived in their own fallen sense of self-worth. He shares that he suffered perils from all aspects of the world. Maybe you haven't been beaten like Paul, but maybe the lashings you have received have been that of the heart and soul. I was with my grandchildren and a few of their cousins just yesterday, as I write this, and one of my grandson's was deeply wounded by the words of his cousin. They are between the ages of 10-14. The fourteen year old cousin said to him with a hate filled authority, "Nobody likes you, not even my mother! You annoy everyone." This left him crushed, thinking that he was almost worthless. My wife and I spent the rest of the day in heart-triage, trying to repair damage to his self-being. He was hurt because he listened to a false and hurtful world and allowed that world to speak into his heart. Worse than that he accepted as truth what was spoken into his heart. There is no question that even when one knows that they are founded in the value of God, those words will still hurt, yet when one is aware of a greater relation-ship, there is an anchor to keep them from being dashed against the stones of hate and power. The reality is that the cousin was speaking out of her own sense of hurt and emotional pain that she had suffered through the years from parents in a dysfunctional marriage. Unless we realize the truth and start speaking the truth into our lives the process of self-inflicted destruction will pass on from one person to another and from one generation to another.

Paul, after all the hurt of heart and pain of the flesh he suffered, continues with these words, "For I am persuaded that neither death nor life, nor angels nor principalities nor powers, nor things present nor things to come, nor height nor depth, nor any other created thing, shall be able to separate us from the love of God which is in Christ Jesus our Lord."[13] What Paul is saying is what you need to realize in your heart – that God is the one actual source of truth and love and He is greater than all of the dysfunction of the world. No matter what the world told Paul he was only going to believe in the truth of God within himself, which is his *God-worth*, and that truth brought him victory in his heart, spirit and mind even when the greatest forces of the world came against him. If my grandson had reflected upon the love of God within him in the presence of Jesus, he would have been assured of his value and not gone into an

---

[13] Romans 8:38-39.

emotional downspin. It is not that he doesn't know the love of the Lord but that center source must be seen as more than love. *It must be realized as our pure source of strength – our truth and certain reality!* There is no question that God is love, but there is more to the dynamic than that. When it comes to God as our strength and source of identity *we must be single focused and true believers.*

How is that done? To help us make this transition let us look at the life of Abram. He is a man that God called out of the land of his people for a special journey – a journey with God. God called Abram out of his old country, away from his family of heritage, to a new place that God would make. Abram was asked to accept this move by faith. *Yes, faith is the key to relationship with God and to your own true self.* It is through committed faith that God is able to do a new thing in your life. It is through true faith that you will realize your potential and not the world's perception of your potential. *The greater your faith, the greater your realization of God-worth within you, the stronger you will be and the more unshakable you will be.* Remember the story of the life of Christy Brown, the writer? The world most likely told him that he was worthless and could only fail since he only had control of his mind and the little toe on his left foot. Yet, he found a source of strength and potential within himself that the world did not see.

What is faith? Faith is an *exercise in focus* that shifts focus away from one's self to a greater power – it is a recalibration of one's inner source of strength. Faith is joining in the movement of God, even when we haven't seen the results of that belief.[14] Faith is becoming one with the radical love of God even when we still have not seen the place that we are being guided towards. Faith is accepting in our hearts that God means all good for us and has the power to cause that good in our lives and we are willing to let go and follow God's will. Abram accepted this principle of God over everything else. Remember that this direct faith in a personal and present God was new to Abram also. Let's take a moment to hear the conversation between God and Abram, "Now the Lord had said to Abram: 'Get out of your country, from your family and from your father's house, to a land that I will show you. I will make you a great nation; I will bless you and make your name great; and you shall be a blessing. I will bless those who bless you, and I

---

[14] See Hebrews 11:1 for a biblical definition of faith.

will curse him who curses you; and in you all the families of the earth shall be blessed.'"[15]

What is happening here that can give us an understanding for our own relationship with God and that will bless and prosper our lives? First, God is calling Abram into a direct personal and interactive relationship, yet it must be by faith and that means hearing God and turning towards the direction that God would have us move, that is the definition of obedience - to hear God's voice and to turn and follow that voice. Abram followed the word of God and history tells us that he was blessed beyond measure. How can we relate to this? God is always speaking to us. God speaks to us in different ways. God speaks though Jesus Christ, His Son and the Holy Spirit. Scripture is the main way that Jesus speaks to us. In the first chapter of the Gospel of John we are told that Jesus is the living Word. We can hear Jesus speak to us through others and through circumstances. He can and often does speak to us directly in our hearts by the presence of the Holy Spirit. He also speaks to us through our devotions and readings of the saints. The main thing to remember is that God is always speaking and that we need to listen.

---

[15] Genesis 12:1-3.

Second, God is calling for Abram to come away from the old, from his family where they have shaped him, from the old voices of his self-image into the new awareness that God will shape for him. Old things must be left and he must become new, yes, new in God with a new perspective and new vision. In other words, you and I must let God reshape our value system just as God did for Abram. By God calling Abram into a new land away from his extended family He is calling Abram into a closer walk with God, to be dependent upon God and to walk in the way of God with God as his major guidance and reflection. In this way God calls each of us into that new type of relationship where our reality is based upon God's presence with us through Jesus Christ and His feelings of love towards us. This is where we find our true worth. Yet, like Abram, we discover it is a *lifelong journey and not an instant fix.*

The teachings throughout Scripture are consistent, we are told of this same reality in 2 Corinthians 5:17, "Therefore, if anyone is in Christ Jesus, he is a new creation; old things have passed away; behold all things have become new." Here we need to keep in mind that though it is spoken of in the masculine it is inclusive of all of God's children – male and female. Think about what is being said! All things can become new! We can leave our old baggage just as Lazarus did in the tomb and as Abram did when God called him out of his old country. When God says, "behold all things have become new" that means that our life is literally *renewed, fresh and starting in the possibilities of God.* Faith brings us to the wonder of this moment in our lives if we are willing to turn to the call of God and to take that first step like Abram did, that is to accept God's will upon our lives, walk with God through the life of Jesus Christ and accept our new identity of being reimaged in the love and truth of Jesus. Think about what I have just said, you can be made new in the "image of Jesus". If you are in the image of Jesus, born anew, afresh, then your core or center of worth becomes the Jesus within you – God-esteem!

It is absolutely possible – if by faith you will accept it! Take a moment right now and contemplate your willingness to accept this truth by faith – not reason, but faith, simple faith as a child would. Reason can come into play later in the process of reflection, but love happens only by faithful release of the heart in response to the initiative of another – yes, it makes us vulnerable but again that is part of faith and part of loving another – *in true love we must always place ourselves at risk!*

Third, out of this new centering of our being in God we will be like Abram, blessed beyond what we have imagined. The words of our self-concept created by the community of the world will no longer place limits upon us. Because of this we will be able to grow in new ways and not be restricted by old voices that tell us we can't do it – Jesus clearly shows us that we can do all things through Him, who strengthens us.[16] *In this way our new center of self-vision begins to come from Jesus and not from ourselves.*

Fourth, notice that God is asserting God's authority over the life of Abram and that the world no longer has authority over Abram. Five times God tells Abram that "I" will do this action in your life – here God speaks with Almighty authority and brings Abram into that unity of God's power. This is the force of grace that God offers over the lives of those who follow in the way of Jesus. *Grace is God's force of goodness freely given to bless your life.* Are you getting a sense of the great and wonderful creating force in the life of one who is willing to take that real step of faith into the way of

---

[16] Philippians 4:13.

Jesus? The truth of faith is, the more you faith into Jesus (using faith as a verb), *the greater will be the results.* The story of Abram demonstrates this clearly.

Two additional events happen in the life of Abram that show the fulfillment that God wants for us in our perspective of new identity. In Genesis 15:1, God speaks again to Abram and brings to fullness this new sense of identity. These words are some of the most profound in all of God's proclamation, "After these things the word of the LORD came to Abram in a vision saying, 'Do not be afraid, Abram, I am your shield, your exceedingly great reward.'" God is inviting Abram to come into unity with Him and then He says Abram will find a new center of strength – God, Himself, will be part of the very core of Abram's being. Notice that God tells Abram not to be afraid that God will in fact be Abram's protection. This promise to Abram is the same promise that Jesus offers to all of God's children. He offers this to you and to me, if we will accept it by faith and *become one with God's radical love in action.* I need to pause at this moment and ask you if you have accepted fully this promise that God is offering you? It is a call for a new and radical orientation of worth. No longer self-directed but *God-centered* and *God-directed!* If this is new to you or if you are already on a journey with Jesus but have not come to fullness by faith, simply open up your heart with sincerity and say, "Lord Jesus please come into my heart and be for me that exceedingly great reward. I need You. I need Your strength and Your reality in my life. I need the fullness of Your love. Forgive me for my slowness to faith. Please come and be my guide." *I assure you that God will not disappoint you.* You may feel something or you may feel nothing immediately, but rest assured, God has moved and He is with you. It is for you to accept this by faith and it will be fulfilled. Imagine God Himself, the Great I AM, is now united with you and is your "exceedingly great reward." Now you can know that all is positive and the old words and thoughts of rejection and limitations are removed and replaced by the force of God Himself who means all goodness for you.

The next conversation between God and Abram that I want you to look at is in Genesis 17:1-7, "When Abram was ninety-nine years old, the LORD appeared and said to him, 'I am Almighty God; walk before Me and be blameless. 'And I will make my covenant between Me and you, and will multiply you exceedingly.' Then Abram fell on his face, and God talked with him, saying: 'As for Me, behold, My covenant is with you, and you shall be a father of many nations. 'No longer shall your name be called Abram, but your name shall be Abraham; for I have made you a father of many nations. 'I will make you exceedingly fruitful; and I will make nations of you, and kings shall come from you. And I will establish My covenant between Me and you and your descendants after you in their generations, for an everlasting covenant, to be God to you and your descendants after you."

Here a fullness of relationship takes place – Abram is now called Abraham, completion is offered him if he will form a bonding of unity with God (covenant). Notice several things, first Abram is ninety-nine years old. Can you imagine the laughter of people if a ninety-nine year old person said that God was going to start a revelation through him and create nations through him? The point for us is that God is now united, one with us and God will do what God will do and that is not formed by human thoughts but by the will and Almighty power of God. Abram accepted this offer and became Abraham – a completion of unity and spirit of will. Then God says, this will not only bring blessings to you but to all of your descendants and the blessings will be "exceedingly" abundant. You will be used to bear fruit for God in relationship with God's children. Now you are no longer formed by the culture of the world but you are freed into the power of God's grace, realizing God's delight for you as God's child. Now your state of mind changes, your attitude changes and you start to think of things in the possibilities of God. This is the transformation that God is offering you. It is the transformation that I realized later in life, many years later after much pain, suffering and hurting from others. Only by meeting Jesus in our hearts can we receive the reality of this promise made to Abraham. Jesus is the fulfillment of that promise. Jesus is in fact, the Promise of God, the "exceedingly great reward." - for those that chose Him by faith. God Himself, in and through Jesus Christ, is your reward as He was the reward for Abraham. He is united within our hearts and souls and becomes our identity and strength. Jesus tells us that we can do all things through Him, but we must believe by faith even if we have yet to see the results. He is absolutely the most positive force in of all creation and now He is united with your heart and spirit. But remember, as God spoke to Abram, "walk before Me", He speaks to us, and we must stay in a faithful relationship. This does not mean that we have to be perfect in everything that we do, but we *must* do our best to be faithful followers of Jesus' will and way of life. That is the key and the staying power, yet do not worry, His grace is there to assist you in that effort – that is part of the exceedingly great wonder of it all.[17]

Apostle Paul found solid ground on this reality of unity with God forming a new identity from within. Abraham was transformed into his human fullness by finding this solid ground. Both became stronger than the world around them and excelled in their potential with God. I also have experienced this amazing potential fulfilled in my life once I realized that I am not merely Gordon inside, but Gordon united with the Spirit of God and the joy is that it is not an equal sharing – as I have turned more and more of my self-will over to God, I have grown greater and greater in His strength, love and truth. It is simply the *physics of God* that as we become less and He becomes more in us, that we in fact become more, even though we become less.[18] But for our purposes here it is important for you to know that your personal being is of God-worth and is formed in the realm of God's infinite love for you and God has the Almighty

---

[17]Ephesians 2:8.
[18] 2Corinthians 12:9.

power to effect God's will in your life as *He is your present helper.*

Jesus Is a God of New Beginnings:

He offers us the reality of exchanging our old worth for His new and eternal worth. The old will be gone and He will fill that space with love, peace and joy and give you the excitement and wonder of His purpose in and through your life. For more under-standing of this see 2 Corinthians 5:17-21; Romans 6:3-8 and Psalm 23.

A Moment of Reflection:

By laying down what is old we can make room for what is new. This may be hard to do but I want you to think of some of the hurtful things that have been said to you, or negative feelings you have about yourself, maybe a negative experience. It could even be feelings of self-doubt, fear or feelings of insufficiency. Remember, these are of the world and you do not have to take ownership of these understandings. They are often given to us by people along our journeys, who themselves are broken and dysfunctional. Often they are just pass-ing along what has been done to them by others, and the brokenness passes from generation to generation.

Intentional Action:

Write each feeling or experience down on a separate small piece of paper. Then I want you to take a candle, light the candle and place a metal pie or cake tin next to the candle and take each piece of paper and hold it over the flame of the candle – *take note of each word or feeling and watch it be extinguished in the flame*. Remember safety first, as you ignite each piece of paper place it into the metal tin, maybe have a cup of water nearby or do this outside of your home. As you see these words which have held you in bondage go up in flame, these negative and untrue perceptions, you have started a process of self-cleansing and healing. Here is the verse from 2Corinthians 5:17, "Therefore, if anyone is in Christ, he or she is a new creation; old things have passed away; behold, all things have become new." Did you hear that? Jesus is wiping away all the false words, all your past mistakes and sins and making you completely new! This is truth if you are willing to accept it by faith! There is no greater gift in all of creation than this gift – the gift of a NEW beginning. It will be as real as you want it to be, empowered by your faith in Jesus. True life is all about Jesus. Only Jesus has the power to cleanse your heart, spirit and soul. I am asking you to read this verse again and realize what it says to your heart – please say it out loud, to yourself. Claim this truth into your being. Make it one with you. This is Jesus' promise to you and He has never broken a promise!

We will continue the process by filling that void which has been created within you, for what has been emptied out of you has left a space and now we must fill it with the presence of Jesus and His love. God loves you infinitely and that means He holds *unlimited* value in His heart for you. If you have ever wondered what was in the heart of God you have just discovered it – you are!

Write Some of Your Thoughts:

How did you feel as you saw those misconceptions of you going up in flames? Are you opening yourself up for God's truth to reshape you? Can you feel the freedom that brings? Are you willing to invite Jesus into that new space within you?

_____

_____

_____

_____

_____

_____

_____

_____

_____

_____

_____

_____

_____

_____

3

Realizing the Need!

Peace I leave with you, My peace I give to you; not as the world gives do I give to you. Let not your heart be troubled, neither let it be afraid.[19]

There are several benefits of finding one's true source of worth. First, it allows you to connect to the true depth and height of your real strength. Second, it gives you a proper perspective to deal with challenges in the world which can at times seem overwhelming – think for a moment, have you felt overwhelmed in the recent past, maybe even today? Third, it will give you a perspective of victory and not defeat, of potential and not despair and one of reality and not falsehood. When someone makes you feel less than worthy you will find your true existence, your true value and it will manifest in true strength to overcome those false

---

[19] John 14:27.

notions. Fourth, it will give you a sense of certainty – absolute certainty in life. Amidst the unknown of the next moment you will have peace and certainty that will be unshakable. *The greatest certainty in the world is uncertainty.* Think about it, our lives are full of the unknown. If your strength is not rooted in absolute truth then you will dwell in fear of that uncertainty and stress will overcome you, fill you with doubt and keep you from reaching your potential. However, finding absolute truth frees us as humans from that stress and fear and brings peace into our hearts and souls.[20] At the core of this personal peace is the reality of who you truly are as a person. Until you find the fullness of that reality you will not have perfect strength, yet when you find it you will discover strength beyond anything you have ever experienced.

Jesus says of Himself, "I am the way, the truth and the life."[21] Notice that in this statement Jesus is reflecting upon the absolute certainty concerning His being – there is no question within

---

[20] Yes, we as humans have hearts with spiritual substance, souls and spirits. For a teaching on this understanding see my writing, *"Seeing Through the Eyes of Heaven"*.
[21] John 14:6.

His being about who He is and His purpose. In this statement Jesus also makes an invitation to us to find that certainty that we need in the inner core of our being – our hearts and souls. If we allow Jesus to dwell within us by faith, then we will have a truth in us that is unshakable. Then when the storms of life come we will not be moved and will be certain about whose we are and who we are. Having that truth within you will give new life and it will be based upon His extreme love for you and this will provide a new path or way of life. In fact in John 10:10, Jesus says exactly what I am sharing with you in this writing, that if we believe what the world tells us we will suffer great limitation, loss and pain, but if we will place Him at the core of our inner-being we will have life and have it "more abundantly".

I was once standing outside a fairly modest home which had been given to me for use by a church family which I was serving. It was mine to use during the period of my service as their pastor. I had left all of my former riches, the large house with the heated swimming pool, indoor spa room and five cars in the driveway and there I was in the middle of the county 15 miles from the nearest small town. This one morning I was standing in the carport with a pastor friend from Kenya, Africa. For a moment I was lamenting the reality that I had almost no worth, material worth that is, and his reply was straight forward and revealing. He said, "You are rich, you are so rich pastor." He was seeing what I either was not looking at or what I could not see. Once he said this it brought me to my senses and I said to him, "You are right, I am very rich." When I heard what he said, at that moment, I looked inside of my being and stopped looking around me for my worth. It was then that I realized that my worth was infinite in its depth and absolute in its truth. Our true worth lies within each of us.[22]

Each human being has a built in need to find their true inner-worth, which will bring them to a sense of inner-peace. Most of us try to build our worth in the physical reality of this world and become disappointed and often turn to despair. The core reality of our worth is even more vital to human function and purpose than a reflection of whether or not we think we are rich – it is the very core of our human fiber that should ultimately

---

[22] Luke 17:20-21.

direct us in everything that we do. Jesus told His disciples as He tells us, "Peace I leave with you, My peace I give to you; not as the world gives do I give to you. Let not your heart be troubled, neither let it be afraid."[23] Jesus understands how important it is for us to be anchored in His reality and for us to find true certainty and stability in this life. He also understood that for His disciples to be most effective and to fulfill their purpose and fullness of life that they must be grounded in this reality of true worth. So it is for us, as Jesus is the great teacher of truth and ultimate reality. It is true that when we trust in false reality we become shaken in our paths of life. We become anxious and stressed. *This is a good measure of how solidly we are anchored in the truth of life, that is, the amount of peace we experience in our hearts and spirits and the lack of anxiousness and stress we feel.*

Let us look at what is one of the best known biblical stories, that of David and Goliath. David was a young boy, possibly 12- 13 years old when he told King Saul that he was going before this giant enemy of the nation of Israel. Saul offered the traditional warrior's armor but it was far too large

---

[23] John 14:27

and heavy for this young boy David. The Bible doesn't tell us the conversation between Saul and David but we can just imagine for it must have been a foolish picture, yet David persevered and kept his belief and focus – because his belief system was not centered upon himself but upon the God of Israel. When he preceded to the battle ground, to meet Goliath, even his brothers who were in the battle camp of Israel laughed and mocked him. That is especially hurtful when your own family mocks and makes fun of you. How did he manage to hold onto his determination and strength? David had become one in his identity with the God of Israel – that is *functional faith!* It is by faith he accepted that God was with him and would not abandon him. This is the benefit of finding one's true source of strength, which is demonstrated by David; he connects to the depth and height of his real strength. It gives him a perspective that is beyond the power of the world in dealing with challenges.

So David proceeded, yes, against all the negative voices and pressures of this extreme worldly situation. Listen to the conversation be-tween King Saul and David, "Then David said to

Saul, "Let no man's heart fail because of him; your servant will go and fight with this Philistine." And Saul said to David, "You are not able to go against this Philistine to fight with him; for you are a youth, and he a man of war from his youth."[24] Certainly not a conversation of encouragement – Saul is saying, "get real in the world child." Yet, David is anchored in his relationship with God as he responds to Saul, "The LORD, who delivered me from the paw of the lion and from the paw of the bear, He will deliver me from the hand of this Philistine."[25] David had a perspective of victory in his inner-spirit based upon the reality of the God who he knew. The despair was on the part of the army of the Israelites and King Saul, but David had certainty for he knew the word of the living God was absolute. Our inner-connection of true God-worth is one with this spirit of victory and inner-peace of direction in life. It allows each of us to have certainty and *Godly stability*. It is truly an attitude changer in life for those who live in doubt or fear. *The benefits of one finding their true self in*

---

[24] 1 Samuel 17:33.
[25] 1Samuel 17:37.

the unity of God's reality, as David did, can be summed up as finding the reality of God's strength within us. It gives us a perspective of hope in dealing with life's challenges, it gives us an attitude of victory and not despair or fear and lastly it anchors us in the reality of Godly certainty and not in the ebbs and flows of this world. Filling our need by making Jesus the core of our inner-being and our inner-truth, we gain absolute certainty in a world of uncertainty. We gain certainty in a world that is constantly shifting and changing. For more understanding in this area see Matthew 7:24-29; Romans 5:1-5 and Psalm 121.

A Moment of Reflection:

Notice that David knew what his one true need in life was – to be centered upon the living reality of God with him and God's faithfulness towards him. Take a moment and reflect upon your own life. How often do you feel anxious or stressed and how do you deal with it? Do you ever doubt yourself or feel afraid? Are you able to go to a source of strength greater than yourself, to give you peace in all circumstances? Remember Jesus has been through it all and He knows how to handle any situation, our challenge is to lean upon

His strength and we can only do that most effectively by finding His living reality within us and making His strength our strength. Think about it, if you had the strength of Jesus how would your world be different?

Intentional Action:

Accept that this power of the presence of Jesus is in fact within you and every time that you are in doubt, say the words of Apostle Paul, who like you faced overwhelming odds in life, "I can do all things through Christ who strengthens me."[26] The more you proclaim it the more you will believe it and the more you believe it the more you will be strengthened in His power within you. Listen to these words from St. Augustine, one of the great teachers of a life with Jesus, "He was within, and we mistakenly sought Him without. Within us all is a slumbering miracle, a latent Christ, a Light, Power, and immediacy with God."[27]

---

[26] Philippians 4:13.
[27] Thomas Kelly, *The Sanctuary of the Soul* (Nashville: Upper Room Books, 1997), 24.

Write Some of Your Thoughts:

How do you think your life would be different if you lived in the faith that David knew? What does the thought of St. Augustine mean to you and your life? How would it change the vision for your life?

_____

_____

_____

_____

_____

_____

_____

_____

_____

_____

_____

_____

4

Reaching for the Richness of Life

"These things I have spoken to you, that My joy may remain in you, and that your joy may be full."[28]

The truth is that God wants the very best for you as you journey through your life's path. However, it is also true that we are affected by our environment which most of the time is less than Godly and is not always filled with goodness or truth. Because we often buy into the reality of the world and not that of Heaven and the present power of Jesus Christ within us, we do not achieve the best that the Lord Jesus has already prepared for us. Did you hear what I said? I want you to think about that statement for a moment, the "best that the Lord has already prepared". That is what the prophet Isaiah spoke about when he said, "but those who wait for the LORD shall renew their

---

[28] John 15:11

strength, they shall mount up with wings like eagles, they shall run and not be weary, they shall walk and not faint."[29] It is a calling for us, as children of God, and we are all children of God, to come into the stream of His present and living *grace* in order to have the fullness of riches that He wants for us. *His riches are already present in grace, we simply need to find the flow of its pattern in the structure of our lives.* Unlike the astronomical chances of you winning the next state lottery, Jesus affords each of us absolute and eternal certainty - simply by the willingness of our hearts to accept His truth and to grow in that reality. *Jesus offers you His assisting grace which will unite with your life and give you Godly help along the path of life.*[30] That is why Jesus came to this earth in physical reality, so that the desire of God for a living and loving relationship with God's children would be known in its fullness. *God is first, most and always about relationship;* relationships that are real,

---

[29] Isaiah 40:31.
[30] Ephesians 2:8, John 14:16 & 15:5.

loving, and fulfilled. Jesus is a God of the *now of life*. God knows well our struggles, our hurts, pain and brokenness and that is why God sent Jesus into the world that we wouldn't have to go it alone. Jesus came to give us the power to fulfill life in this place and to know life with Him forevermore. John 3:16, tells us why, "For God so loved the world that He gave His only begotten Son that whoever would believe in Him would not perish but have everlasting life." It is God's nature that *He so loves* – let me say that again, *God so loves*. He so loves you that He is willing to sacrifice Himself for you. He so loves you that nothing in Heaven or on earth will stand between Him and His love for you.[31] He so loves you that His love is absolute – in other words, there is nothing that you can do to make Him love you more and there is nothing that you can do to make Him love you less – that is true love. Yes, His heart hurts when we don't get it right, and He may be disappointed with us at times but His love never stops and it is always complete in its desire for us to be made whole and full of joy. He tells us that He did not come to judge us or condemn us – no, not at all. He came to help us.

---

[31] Romans 8:37-39.

John 3:17 says, "God sent His Son into the world, not to condemn the world, but that the world might be saved through Him." Do you see the difference between the voice of God and the voice of the world? God speaks to enhance, to direct us into fullness of life, to heal our wounds and to give each of us true life from NOW to FOREVER! You need to stop right now and think about that last understanding – *true life for now and forever*, that's the ultimate gift. That is why I say to you, Jesus is the God of the *now of life*. In John 3:17, the word "save" in Greek has two meanings, first, the understanding of bringing one into true life and complete relationship with God. Second, it means to be healed, healed from the wounds of the words and destructive voices and actions of this world. We, as broken humans, must be saved to be healed and healed to be saved – they go together in God's grace of restoration. God is certain about His desire – the very best for you, but it is our decision that God waits upon – will you say yes to Jesus and let Him give you the *God-assistance* that you need?

Let me share a story with you. It is said that Constantine was with his army in the mountains of

48

Eastern Europe and they needed to get to the other side of the mountain ridge but there was no easy way of passage. A tunnel was spotted and it appeared to go through the mountain to the other side. It was dark in the tunnel, as it was very long and deep. Constantine took a risk and led his army in that pathway. As they were going through this tunnel they often had to hold onto the person in front of them in order to stay on the path because it was so dark. During their walk through this abyss they heard a voice and it said, "Pick it up, pick it up!" Well, considering their fatigue and lack of sight, many responded by ignoring the voice or what they thought was a voice. Some reached down with one hand and while holding onto the person in front of them grabbed what they could. There were others who reached down and grabbed what they could with both hands and filled their pockets to overflowing. As they continued in that darkest of paths there appeared a light at the end of the tunnel. When they came to the opening and they could see in the light, they realized what they had or didn't have. Those who reached down and grabbed what they could at the bidding of the voice, saw that they had in their hands rubies, pearls, diamonds and gold.

Those that didn't respond to the command were despondent and wept, those who reached down with one hand were sorrowful that they hadn't given more effort and belief to the command and those who filled their pockets to fullness were rejoicing and celebrating. The riches of full and joyful life are within our reach if we will but respond to the invitation of Jesus. Each soldier in that cave realized that they had a need. They were all trying to get to the other side, where there was light and where they could fulfill their purpose. Yet, there were those who didn't benefit from the truth that would enhance their *present* and *future* journey. There were those who, despite being in a strange environment, heard the voice of truth and responded appropriately and were blessed beyond measure. There are those in life who continue in their old ways and suffer the sorrows of that decision, but there are those who have listened to that greater voice and have found the path for their fulfillment. Each of us has a need to be made whole and complete, to travel this journey with certainty and not be in fear. Maybe right now Jesus is calling out to you, "Pick it up, pick it up!" Maybe He is saying this is your opportunity to be filled with joy and infinite riches. Like those men in the cave, our path can seem dark at times, but Jesus is always calling out to us and trying to guide us towards prosperity and abundance of life. The word of Jesus is the richness that He wants you to receive, greater than any gem, he offers it to you freely for your taking, just as those men were offered to freely pick up what was on the ground of the cave. Some ignored the offer, some partially responded and some responded wholeheartedly. How will you respond?

Let's again hear these words from the prophet Isaiah and consider what it would be like in our lives if we lived the reality of these words. What would it be like if these words came to fullness for each of us?

But those who wait on the LORD
Shall renew their strength;
They shall mount up with wings like eagles,
They shall run and not be weary,
They shall walk and not faint.[32]

---

[32] Isaiah 40:31

Can you imagine that in your daily life that you could be strong enough to handle any situation and "not be weary" or "faint"? Can you imagine that even in the midst of the power and struggles of the world you can feel the lightness of your spirit as if you where soaring on the wing of an eagle?

Can you imagine that you can have control and are not being controlled by the lowly forces of this world which have already attempted to deceive you and to confuse you? Well, it is all possible but you must learn to have a different vision – *you simply must refocus your vision.* You must be willing to let go of the vision that others have given you of yourself for the vision that God has for you. His is a far greater vision of your ulti - mate possibility in life – a life rich in goodness and joy. These words from Isaiah are possible for you and are the affirming words that God wants you to hear. It is a new vision from within which will change your life both inwardly and outwardly.

Making Room for Joy in Our Lives:

Like those soldiers in the cave, the more of Jesus Christ that we bring into our inner-being, the more joy we have and the more strength we have. This is the good news of Jesus Christ and it is given to us through His living revelation in the word of God – specifically, in the New Testament. Like those soldiers, continue to "pick it up" and bring it into yourself. It will make you rich now and forever. For further reference see John 17:13-26.

A Moment of Reflection:

In the previous chapter you have already laid down the old and made room for the new. Like those soldiers, it's time to pick up what is new, open up to that "new voice" and to receive the blessings. What God sees in you is a beautiful creation that only He could weave together. Once you start to understand this and recalibrate your perspective and vision of reality then the shift into new found riches of worth will take place.

Intentional Action:

Write some of the most positive things that have been said to you. Write what the most loving God would want you to think of yourself. If you find it hard to do, then try writing this "God who is perfect love, means all good for me. He has created me to know His love for me" and then write what that perfect love and goodness means for you. It may simply mean that "I accept that Jesus loves me perfectly and I can see that truth as I look at the cross and realize that He died just for me, as He did for all." Give it a try.

Write Some of Your Thoughts:

You may want to write the words that you accept into your true nature – remember, your true nature comes from the source of perfect love.

_____

_____

_____

_____

_____

_____

_____

_____

_____

_____

_____

5

The Great Shift – Discovering Your Real Self

"And you shall know the truth, and the truth shall make you free."[33]

I thought I had broken free of that spirit of failure that was cast upon me by that guidance counselor that day, but the truth is that it had become part of my being. It manifested in my self-doubt throughout my life –at least until the years of my middle age. It was only when I had an encounter with the person of Jesus that I was able to transition from brokenness to a state of reconstruction and then into a state of being healed and filled with joy. I think that a proper road sign for my journey of life would now be "Drive with Caution - Work in Progress" and that will be the case until I enter that final glory with Jesus

---

[33] John 8:32.

Christ. *Once we make the shift to that greater reality within us we must be mindful of the fallen world around us and that it still can cause us harm.*

For at least half of my life I was a walking bundle of insufficiency. Because of that I turned to trying to please others and to please the culture that I found myself in at any given moment. I became an instrument of the culture and lost myself in the process. *The reality is that I didn't have any real roots growing my own true nature that was given of God.* Please read that again – and I want to ask you where are your roots, what are you tapping into for your strength and nourishment? Take a moment to think about this, be real with yourself, it's only between you and God. Listen to these words from God in the revelation of God's reality for His children from the First Psalm: "Blessed is the man or woman who walks not in the counsel of the ungodly, nor stands in the path of sinners, nor sits in the seat of the scornful; but their delight is in the law of the LORD, and in His law they will meditate day and night. They shall be like a tree planted by the rivers of water, that brings forth its fruit in its season, whose leaf also shall not wither; and whatever they do shall prosper."

Did you know that most trees have a 'tap root'? There is a surface root system that lies just beneath the ground surrounding the tree, its purpose is to receive the surface water – that is the water that doesn't run deep. This surface root system is necessary for life of the tree but it will not be able to maintain the life of the tree in times of drought or even mild shortage of water. If it doesn't rain for a week or two (which is not a long time) the tree would be at a loss to gain its life sustaining fluid. The tap root is the root of the tree that directs itself to grow straight down into the depth of the earth and to be the main source of nourishment for the tree – to sustain it in good times and bad times. It is the anchor of hope for the tree that if things get bad on the surface it will have a source that will carry it through that dry period. Like a tree planted by "rivers of water" which is constantly fed its sustaining nourishment, when we tap into the deeper source of our true being we are revived, replenished and re-nourished. Have you ever been thirsty and couldn't wait until you got a drink of water to quench your thirst – of course you have. That is the inner feeling of your heart and soul when you don't tap deep into the reality of that infinite source of life – the source of pure love and life itself. Have you felt it, it is a feeling of need within you, maybe we could call it, a void or emptiness. Note that the person who wrote this psalm finds their true source of life, "They will be like a tree planted by rivers of water, that brings forth its fruit in its season." Here that source is one's relationship with God and the person delights in that living relationship and desires for it to be real, deep and fulfilling. It is necessary to understand this because the reality of the world won't change but you can change, you can take authority over the false powers of the world by tapping deep into the eternal truth of God. First, that God's love for you through Jesus Christ is unwavering and certain, and second, that it is an assisting presence in your life to *lead you into a right, healing and prosperous path*, as the Psalmist says, "and whatever they do shall prosper."[34] In my own journey I didn't yet realize this truth so the false and hurtful powers of the

---

[34] This is taken from Psalm 1 in the NKJ and is paraphrased to be inclusive of all of God's children.

world still had authority over me. We must remember that the false powers of the world are constantly exerting their forces of oppression against us. Each day as we go out into the world to work, travel and interact we encounter the negative forces of the world. This interaction of power between us and the world is directly addressed by the psalmist in Psalm 119:133, "Direct my steps by Your word, and let no iniquity have dominion over me. Redeem me from the oppression of man, that I may keep Your precepts." The person who wrote this understood the struggle between what the world tells us and that which God tells us. If we are not aware of this or we don't use it for our good then we will be tossed about by the waves on the sea of emotions and when difficulties arise we will be confused and in a crisis mode.

Before finding the certainty of the positive power of Jesus Christ in my life I would often join in the voices that made fun or belittled other people. If I could lower them in their sense of worth then I could feel better about myself and my own little sense of worth. I turned to the false pleasures of the world. I indulged in obsessive work, drinking and excessive materialism thinking that if I followed those paths within my life I would find the strength and value that I personally did not possess. I thought there was power in drinking, work and material riches, to mention only a few of the straws that I reached for in my grasp to find true strength, but truly they were only objects hanging around my neck and they took what worth I had and depleted it further. Being real with yourself, what things do you grab onto along the way of life to find your strength? If it is not God-centered then it is a false and destructive presence in your life. Give it some thought. [35]

That guidance counselor's voice wasn't the only measure of my worth that I carried around with me for a good part of my life, there were many more voices in my inner being telling me I should live in fear and apprehension, that I was not as good as others. Sometimes the voices were not

---

[35] We must understand that sex and work are not bad in and of themselves. They are created by God for our good, yet they can be misused and even abused. It is only through God and the reality of His love in our hearts that we reach the fulfillment of true human relationship. This includes all aspects of our lives including those of work and sex.

as direct as that guidance counselor, sometimes they came cloaked in an expression of care and friendship and sometimes they came from those closest to me. *If we do not know genuine Truth then what is false will become real for us and we will live in false awareness and see that as true life* – which is ultimately a lie. It is in this way that we place ourselves under the authority of others.

Think about Christy Brown, the author which Sol Stein told us about. He learned to type with his one toe, one letter at a time, one touch and beat of one toe repeatedly receiving the thrust of his strength. The negative messages that the world had told him he defied: "You are not whole.", "You cannot be anything.", "You are less than human." The ultimate truth is that he showed the world what true humanity is about. It is not about our flesh in the forms that culture tells us is necessary – the perfect waves of the hair, the TV selected curves of the body or the crowd pleasing acts of self-belittlement of others for the enhancement of one's own pleasure. Christy shows us that there is something deeper in the inner-being of oneself which is greater than the power of the outer being or the flesh. There, somewhere within each of us is a source of inner presence or strength, of who we can be over and against all the untruth of the words that we carry around our necks as oppressive baggage.

Like Christy, I had a mother who tried to speak truth into me, but unlike Christy I didn't listen closely enough. I remember the times that I would come home from school as a child, maybe in middle school, feeling so low about myself and there I sat at the kitchen table as my mother was busy making dinner or one of her delicious desserts – she was so loving. She would tell me I was worthy and I could do what I set my mind to and then she would speak her trump card into the conversation, "God is with you and He has created you in His image." Well I thought I couldn't be all bad if I had some of that in me – but where was it and why did I hurt so inside?

In sixth grade we were told by our teacher, Mr. Strong, that there was going to be in a writing competition that would be district wide and the winner would receive a prize. We were to write our autobiography. We all had to give it a try. I again was positioned at that place of the kitchen table telling my mother, who was busy at her motherly work, I couldn't do it! She refused to accept my defeat and spoke life into me with her words of love and hope. I told her I didn't have any knowledge of what my life was like when I was born. She proceeded to tell me of her experience of carrying me into the hospital and the conditions of that cold winter night in mid-January. I wrote as she spoke and then inter-mixed my own thoughts and completed it. I took the paper in and submitted it and quickly forgot about it. Weeks passed then one day there was a strange commotion in our classroom. Someone came to the door of the classroom and asked Mr. Strong to come out into the hallway. Then a few minutes later he opened the door, stuck his head in the opening and called out my name and asked me to come out into the hallway. This was not a good feeling for me – when you naturally feel less than worthy – less than human, you don't want any situation to focus upon you – in fact you simply want to be unnoticed. There I stood looking up into faces of strangers and I could feel their voices of condemnation, "Who wrote this for you?", the voice billowed down at me. I replied in truth, "No one." "You are lying." I was told. "You are not capable of writing this good." Then the next voice said, "Your mother wrote this didn't she?" I said, "No." It would have been easier to tell them yes, that was what they wanted to hear. It is true that I had to ask my mother what it was like when I was born – I certainly didn't know, but isn't that the start of good writing, seeking sources of truth? At that point Mr. Strong had had enough of seeing one of his students abused so painfully and forcefully. He defended me and was clearly overflowing with indignation. He ushered me away from them, maybe thinking that they had done enough harm, and we reentered the classroom where he, in his well meaning way and overflowing anger, proceeded to tell the class what had happened. This compounded my feeling of worthlessness, since I was just told that I could not have possibly written that paper. Again, there was a knock at the door and Mr. Strong was called outside. He returned to present me with my prize, as he expressed, begrudgingly given to me by those who didn't want me to receive anything. It was a yellow, unsharpened #2 wooden pencil. He apologized to me and to the class, but the damage was done, it was confirmed in my mind, I ultimately was a failure. Those voices in the hallway were carried throughout the years and culminated in the office of that guidance counselor, reminding me, "You are a failure!"

If any person looks into their hearts and is truthful with themselves each will find voices of negativity that have been poured out upon them. The question becomes how will one find the truth to overcome these false words? How will you find your true self in the midst of false teachings?

For me, after years of self-abuse and misguided exploitation of substances from material to mental, something life changing happened, I met the person named Jesus. It is true. I met Him in the interior of my being. After years of reflection I can say that He was there all the time waiting and hoping for me to discover Him. When I say, "I met the person Jesus.", I am not speaking meta-phorically or in hyperbole, but in truth and reality. Jesus is a real and living presence in the lives of those who accept Him and are willing to open their hearts to Him. He even had spoken out to me in the voice of my mother, in the protective indignation of Mr. Strong, who like a paternal guard sought to stand in defense of me between the corrupting nature of fallen humanity and truth. It was the finding of Jesus within me that gave me the knowledge of discernment in which I finally could distinguish the voices that were of Jesus and those which were of the world.

These stories I have shared with you about myself are illustrations of the negative force in the world which is given by those who do not know the truth about the love of Jesus which resides in each human heart waiting to be discovered. Once His presence within our being is discovered we will be set free. Once set free into this new reality, our vision will be on our true source of worth and not upon the limited and hurtful vision of others and instead of perpetuating words of destruction into lives of others we will speak words of life and encouragement – that is the flow of grace, life with the living Jesus.

In the life of Jesus and the teachings of the Bible there are only two major motions, or movements of force in and through God for His children and that is forward and upward; *forward,* into the greater love of Jesus and His likeness within each of us, and *upward*, into a higher level of consciousness of His infinite power within each of His children. Unlike the voices of the world Jesus is calling out to tell you that you are His beloved, that you are His treasure and that He has His fulfillment planned for your life and if you walk with Him and let Him walk with you, it cannot and will not be denied!!!

Hear some of what Jesus has to say about you, His relationship with you and your potential. First, listen to these words of uplifting truth, of intimate closeness and love for your being as spoken by the psalmist. Let them be your perspective, "For You formed my inward parts; You covered me in my mother's womb...Your eyes saw my substance, being yet unformed. And in Your book they all were written, the days fashioned for me, when as yet there were none of them."[36] Then He goes on to say, "For I know the thoughts that I think toward you, says the LORD, thoughts of peace and not of evil, to give you a future and a hope. Then you will call upon Me and go and pray

---

[36] Psalm 139:13,16.

to Me, and I will listen to you. And you will seek Me and find Me, when you search for Me with all your heart." [37] This approaches a high point in the wish that Jesus has for each of us, as His children. He delights in you as a perfect loving parent would and expresses that delight with these words, "being confident of this very thing, that He who has begun a good work in you will complete it until the day of Jesus Christ." [38]

Are you sensing the difference in these words spoken by Jesus and the negative words of the world as displayed by the pre-disposition given to someone like Christy Brown or the words that shattered my own young understanding of self-worth? What I am about to say to you is an *eternal truth,* there is not one speck of negativism in Jesus; Jesus is pure, complete good and perfect love and He means the very best for you. So when I met Him and discovered that He is alive and within me, then there was a *great shift* that took place. This great shift in reality that moved me, can move anyone who connects to this one true force of life. Jesus

---

[37] Jeremiah 29:11-13.
[38] Philippians 1:6; my paraphrase of the final segment of that verse.

will move you from self-worth, to *God-worth*, from self-esteem to *God-esteem,* from unworthiness to wholeness, from a broken spirit to wondrous love, from fear to optimism, from defeat to hope, from inadequacy to being fulfilled and most of all from sadness to joy!

There was a young girl that once came to a church that I served. She is someone that I learned to care for and love as a good father would. Her life had not been easy, in fact how she survived to that point in her teenage years was itself an act of God. Her story is not unlike millions of stories in our human family. In the false way of life people use their power over others to exploit and build up their own power and sense of worth; making others feel inadequate so they can increase their sense of self-worth. If a person does not have their worth based upon the truth of Jesus then they seek to create their own center and concept of worth which is ultimately built upon the negative and false teachings they have received from the world – the cycle keeps repeating itself. The first time I met her she said something to me that has stayed in my spirit throughout the years. It was a Sunday morning and I was getting ready for service, she entered my office and said she wanted to join the church family. I was a bit taken back as it seemed that she should get to know us better before making such a major decision. I asked her why she felt that our family should be the one she should join and she, in a quiet meekness said, "I was here last week when you were out of town and I have been to other churches but here I feel the presence of *peace."* The true meaning of the word peace as used by Jesus means realizing a level of completeness in love and acceptance, as only Jesus can provide. This connected presence within one's heart and soul replaces fear and apprehension with loving comfort and certainty of eternal strength. I am not sure that she understood it in that defined way, but that is what she was expressing. She was saying, "I have seen all the pain that the world has poured upon me and I am hurting so bad within me, but in this place I can feel a shift of what is true and I want to turn from what is false to what is true." What she felt in that place was greater than the bricks and mortar, the beautiful stained-glass windows, the loving faces – she sensed the living presence of Jesus Himself. I later learned of her deep hurt and pain in the young years of her life, but in that moment in my office she witnessed to the reality that Jesus had opened a door for her and she wanted to walk through it – into His waiting and loving arms, and she did just that. She became a vibrant and joyful member of our faith family and an encouragement and joy to all of us. It took time but it started with the felt presence of positive love and peace that she first connected with.

For some of us it may be less extreme, but nevertheless it is a shift that must be made in order to come to the greater being that Jesus wants for us. Jesus is first and foremost about relationship and you are at the core of His desire. He longs for you and thirsts for a real and loving relationship with you. Jesus said this from the cross in the Gospel of John, 19:28, "I thirst!" He is completely about relationship and you are at the center of His heart. This is the first step to healing and wholeness and it comes by faith. It can't be purchased, it can't be pulled off the shelf of the grocery store, you simply have to give yourself to

Him in faith and He will do the rest, It is that simple, yet our human nature has been so tainted and distorted by the words of untruth that have been poured out upon us, we resist, thinking something that good cannot be real. Simply let go and give in to Jesus and the wonder of your true worth will shine forth in living hope.

A young man found himself in our church family by way of a friend. He at first seemed a bit rough, like an unpolished stone. Getting to know him I found out that at the age of 17 he had been in jail nearly twenty times. As I met with him I shared what I am sharing with you, that if we accept what the world tells us we will be subject to its hurt, pain and depression and there will be no end to that degree of hurt and pain. I explained to him exactly what I am saying here, that our true worth is discovering that Jesus dwells in each of us and His love for us is infinite and He tells us that we are worthy and wondrously made in His image and that He will always be with us, never to leave us or forsake us.[39] When anchored in that reality a shift in our inner being takes place. He experienced this

---

[39] Hebrews 13:5.

reality over a period of several months and found that what other people had said to him was out of their own hurt and insufficiency and he realized he did not have to own their problems. He had found truth, in the perfect love of Jesus within himself. I explained to him that he need only listen to Jesus, for Jesus is life and truth, grace and love. It is Jesus who speaks life into His children if they are willing to listen. One of the last times I saw him he came bounding down the hallway of the church, beaming and enthusiastically proclaiming to me that he was sold out. I said "What do you mean you are sold out?", he responded, "I have given myself wholly to Jesus and I couldn't be happier." All his years of hearing authority figures telling him that he was no good, a failure, a blight upon society, had come to a wall, a wall of truth against which these false teachings could not penetrate, they fell into shattered pieces of their own nothingness and this wall was like no other that he had ever seen – it amazingly started to move and enfold him in arms of loving comfort and acceptance. My friend, do you know these arms, these arms that reach out in loving acceptance, these arms that give perfect assurance and protection? This young man was now allowed to see the world and others through new eyes – the eyes of Jesus. A shift had taken place in His life and vision, *he had been recreated!*

As Jesus walked the earth – He also had to deal with voices of negativity. Listen to this short conversation between the disbelieving Jews and Jesus, "'Do we not say rightly that You are a Samaritan and have a demon?' Jesus answered, 'I do not have a demon; but I honor My Father, and you dishonor Me.'"[40] We must be reminded that the Jews were His own people and they rejected Him. How painful that must have been for Him? Rejection is the greatest pain a human can experience, yet each day it takes place among people, between friends, married couples, parents and children and children towards their parents – it is a disease that is passed on and if not checked will destroy and disfigure. Maybe you have experienced this form of pain – the words of others saying you are not wanted, not included and are just too different. Yet, notice Jesus' response. He speaks life and truth into the situation. He says exactly what I shared with that 17 year old boy and

---

[40] John 8:48-49.

am sharing with you, "I honor My Father". In other words Jesus is saying that I receive the awareness of My being from My Father and not from you. Jesus said I know who I am, I am the substance of the Father and that can't be changed – not by anyone's word. What you say to Me has no bearing on who I am, for My truth and My being comes from the perfect love of My Father. By Jesus maintaining His active relationship with the heavenly Father, He was not under the authority of the false and demeaning words of those who chose to hurt Him, but under the arms of the love and truth of His perfect Father. Jesus shows us the way of the shift in our reality and the force and power of such a shift. Notice in this shift that Jesus is focused first, foremost and always upon the living dynamic connection to the Father. It is possible for us to do the same. We are to look to Jesus for our true reality and this is to be our living dynamic of life. By His living word stirred into our hearts He will speak truth into us and guide us. In the Gospel of John chapter 14:16-17 Jesus says, "And I will pray the Father, and He will give you another Helper, that He may abide with you forever – "the Spirit of truth, whom the world cannot receive, because it neither sees Him nor knows Him; but you know Him, for He dwells with you and will be in you." See, the very Spirit of God will come and dwell with you in this life – Jesus is not talking about the hereafter, but the *NOW* of life. And Jesus says that this Spirit of God will be "with you and will be in you." and will be your "Helper". He also says that the Spirit of God will lead you in truth and then He acknowledges that the world does not know this truth or live this truth. He is the only one who can put truth in the hearts of God's children. It is this truth of your true potential that will lift you up and carry you forward with joy in your heart.

We must remember – Jesus is willing to be engaged in our lives, He is ever-present in our lives and He has absolute and perfect love for us. He means all good for us, and will cause the very best for us. That is not to say that we won't have hard times but He will ultimately see us through.

In Jesus is Positive Power: Jesus is willing to share His positive power with you in your journey of life. There is no negative spirit in Him, only positive. As you get to know Him you will grow in that positive power that He will freely give you.

For more understanding on this thought read the 8th chapter of the Gospel of John and reflect up who Jesus really is, and how He wants to set each of us free.

A Moment of Reflection:

Can you relate to what I have shared with you about voices that put you down, that don't call out the best in you? It can be an everyday occurrence. It may take place at work, in school among those loose and wild tongues of pain or it may be as close as home, where the heart is most vulnerable. Wherever you encounter this reality of a less then true existence, I want you to remember the words of Jesus to your heart and soul, "These things I have spoken to you, that in Me you may have peace. In the world there is tribulation; but be of good cheer, I have overcome the world".[41] Look to the Cross of Jesus – all of the rejection and hurt that the world could muster in one place came together against Jesus. *The great shift of eternal reality is that Jesus overcame all of this.* He defeated death itself and that is the greatest negative force in all of creation and He did this that you can also have this victory when you join in

---

[41] John 16:33.

unity with Him. Remember, the world will never stop its negative assault against you but you can be equipped to recognize it for what it is and to deal forthrightly with it - this is the message of Jesus' ultimate love for YOU!

Intentional Action:

Just maybe, going through your day, when the words of untruth and destruction are spoken towards you, try saying quietly to yourself, "I can do all things through Christ who strengthens me!"[42] Or "If God is for us, who can be against us?"[43]

It is alright to personalize this verse and use the first person, "If God is for me, who can be against me." In fact that is what God wants you to realize. These are just my suggestions to help you get started. Choose an appropriate Bible verse – there is *living power in the word of God*. May I suggest Psalm 91, especially verses 1-4 and 14-16. Repeat it over and over and watch your spirit change and swell with strength, joy and happiness

---

[42] Philippians 4:13.
[43] Romans 8:31.

within. This is called a "breath prayer".[44] A breath prayer is a prayer that is quietly said within one's self repeatedly throughout the day. It can even be said as one is encountering others. It will give you great strength. It will give you the sense of standing with God in the midst of others.

Isn't it interesting that we, as humans, often give all of our time and thought to words that are far less than worthy of our being, yet we often don't take time to speak truth into our being. This is a way to speak truth into your being – take the time, make the time – for you are the one whom the God of all creation has said when He created you, "You are My child made in the image of My goodness and I will fulfill My purpose in you!"

Write Some of Your Thoughts:

Think of some words you have heard during the day and how you responded – it could be interpersonal or from your social network or even from the media. We do not pick up negative thoughts only from interpersonal relationships but throughout our interactions with the culture in

---

[44] The understanding of this type of prayer was given to us by John Cassian. He was one of the Desert Fathers of the Fourth Century.

which we live. Do you need to make an adjustment
in your life?

_____

_____

_____

_____

_____

_____

_____

_____

_____

_____

_____

_____

6

A Shift in Focus: Enhancing Your Future

"I am the light of the world. Whoever follows Me will not walk in darkness, but have the light of life."[45]

Think of the reality of Jesus, He faced many seemingly impossible situations. He entered into a world of such brokenness, of such hurt, pain and rejection, "He was in the world, and though the world was made through him, the world did not recognize him. He came to that which was his own, but his own did not receive him." In the face of the untruth of the world Jesus was willing to speak truth. He spoke truth into the present powers of both the established religious structure and the Roman occupation. His task was of Godly proportions – *to show us the way to shift our focus to the source of His strength so that we could share*

---

[45] John 8:12.

His strength.. We must ask ourselves how He managed this, being fully human; having a shared nature like ours? Certainly He was also fully divine, but He shared our human nature that so often pulls us into its weakness. If we can understand how Jesus bolstered His Spirit to stay focused upon His true reality in the face of so many voices telling Him He wasn't who He proclaimed to be, including His own family, then maybe we would find *the true building block* for our own present strength.

Even as a young boy Jesus faced condemnation and disbelief of His true nature. Maybe just like you? During one Passover celebration His parents discovered He was missing and went looking for Him. He was twelve years old at the time and they naturally had heartfelt concern for Him. They found Him in the Temple dialoguing with the religious teachers. Eugene Peterson, in *The Message*, paraphrases the conversation this way, "Young man, why have you done this to us? Your father and I have been half out of our minds looking for you." He said, "Why were you looking for me? Didn't you know that I had to be here, dealing with the things of my

Father? But they had no idea what he was talking about."[46] Here Jesus gives us the first glimpse of how He dealt with life in a negative environment. His mental and spiritual focus, were centered upon His true Heavenly Father. His first priority was to stay centered upon the true source of His strength and to receive the reinforcement from this source of pure love and truth. Even His parents didn't understand His true reality, but He made a decision and chose this path for His life. Jesus was experiencing a shift in reality, if not a shift at the least a manifestation or magnification of reality – possibly all three. For Jesus at the age of twelve this shift was an intensification of who He knew He truly was. It wasn't easy for Him as we read in Scripture – so many voices of criticism, *but He listened to His heavenly Father of love, the voice of eternal encouragement, the voice of true and certain relationship.* My friend, what voice are you listening to? Are you listening to God's voice? Jesus says, "You are My Beloved, and you hold the potential of My image; My grace and truth." Are you ready to make that shift?

---

[46] Luke 2:48-50.

What Jesus has shown us and is teaching us is that we can have His eternal light and love within our being too, if we but chose to look to the true source of our greatness. The psalmist declared this truth in many ways, but none more clearly than when he spoke for the Lord with these words, "I will instruct you and teach you in the way you should go; I will guide you with My eye."[47] If God places this much emphasis upon the nature of vision shouldn't we? It is the true path to entering greatness. *What we focus upon in life is the ultimate influence of what we will become.* If we are not aware of the power of Jesus within us, then it is possible that what we will become is what the voices of culture tell us.

Jesus focused upon the Heavenly Father and fulfilled His purpose of building a new bridge between the Father and His hurting children. By His focus He was able to offer reconciled healing to a broken relationship between humanlike and God. There was no greater example of Jesus' intentional focus than the Cross. In this way Jesus teaches us the core to healing and being made whole. He

---

[47] Psalm 32:8.

focused upon His Heavenly Father and was able to overcome all worldly powers – even death.

Jesus is calling out for each of us to have Him as the focus of our lives and then we will more clearly understand our true nature – *that you are created in goodness, godliness and are eternally special.* Maybe this teaching is new to you, it is not as the world tells us, but as Jesus tells us, that yes, we can be healed and heal others; yes, we can be given His strength that goes beyond measure, that we can guide and help others; yes, we can receive words of life into our being so that we can speak life into others. Once we choose Jesus as our source of life and strength, center upon His infinite goodness and His willingness to share His likeness with us, *then we form our true identity.* Jesus tells us "And in that day, you will know that I am in My Father, you in Me and I in you."[48] That is the summation of true defined humanity – when we live in the full recognition that Jesus is united with us and that His love and truth reflects out from us as our source of true reality. This is where we start to recognize our true image. *This is where we start*

---

[48] John 14:20.

to be reimaged and are recreated from the defeat of those broken words spoken into our lives and we start to listen to the truth that *infinite greatness is the substance of our true nature.*

In the Book of Daniel we are told of the many gifts that Daniel received from God, gifts of interpreting dreams and visions. It is stressed that Daniel was recognized to have the Spirit of the Holy God with him.[49] Because of this the king favored Daniel and gave him authority over the land, second only to the king. As human nature is consistent, then and now, there were those who were jealous and envious and wanted Daniel removed from power and destroyed. These leaders formed an agreement to move against Daniel and convinced the king to sign a royal decree that anyone who worshiped a god or king other than King Darius for a period of 30 days, would be cast into the den of lions.[50] Daniel, being a Jew, worshiped the one true God and was accused by those that sought his life. The king had signed the decree and could not change the royal order. As

---

[49] Daniel 5:11.
[50] Daniel 6:1-8.

much as the king liked Daniel and as much as the king didn't want to do this to Daniel, he had no choice. The king ordered Daniel to be placed in the lion's den. The next day the king went to the den of lions and cried out to Daniel, and to his amazement Daniel was still living. As the king proclaimed the power of Daniel's God, Daniel told the king, "My God sent His angel and shut the lions' mouths". This is a story about the natural hurtful nature of the unbridled human spirit and it is also part of a much greater story that is the power that comes out of a faithful relationship with God.

Daniel was a man of immense faith and obedience. When he was in the lion's den his concentration and focus was not on being in the lion's den but on God. He placed all of his strength and energy upon God. This focus upon God in effect placed Daniel outside the realm of the power of the lion's den. Yes, Daniel was physically in the den with the lions, however, spiritually he was connected to the living God by the strength of his focus. *Focus is the key catalyst in our lives that will determine our spiritual composition*. Had Daniel not focused so greatly and intensely upon God with his spiritual vision, the lions would have consumed him, however, by his focusing upon God it removed Daniel away from the authority of the lions – he was in effect in union with God.

Somewhere in Daniel's life he made a shift in his reality and that caused him to make a shift in his operative focus. *By faith we are called to make a shift in our reality and by focus we place that reality into motion.* King David, as he reflected upon his life and relationship with God knew the power of focus also, he said, "I foresaw the LORD always before my face, for He is at my right hand, that I may not be shaken. Therefore my heart rejoiced, and my tongue was glad; moreover my flesh also will rest in hope. For You will not leave my soul in Hades, nor will You allow Your Holy One to see corruption. You have made known to me the ways of life; You will make me full of joy in Your presence."[51]

Those words, "I foresaw the LORD always before my face" tell us of the intentionality that David had when it came to his relationship with God. As a young boy when he faced Goliath his

---

[51] Acts 2:25-26; this is referred to from Psalm 16.

vision was not upon Goliath but upon the God with him and within him. It also tells us that focus upon the One true source of life is a *means* to accomplish ultimate joy in one's life. David is giving us a great teaching and it confirms what I am offering you – *focus is the foundational structure for all of life.* We all focus upon something in life as we go from moment to moment, and from day to day. King David's understanding of the power of focus is what carried him in the good times and through the bad. In Psalm 121, he gives us his pronounced need for that ability to focus upon the Lord above all other things. Like you and I he also had troubles in the world that came to unsettle his life. Listen to these words as he finds himself in the midst of life's struggle, "I will lift up my eyes to the hills – from where comes my help?" What he is saying here is exactly our response in the midst of problems or disasters – when we are overwhelmed. What do I do? Who do I turn to? David doesn't look to a friend or to his own means, but he looks up to the hills – which is a metaphor for focusing upon God. Then the next line tells us the outcome, "My help comes from the LORD, who made heaven and earth." I believe that David wrote this second line in reflection, after the occurrence of the threat and its resolution. What he is ultimately saying is, focus upon the Lord, go to Him and He will not disappoint you. We must remember that Jesus is the living God, present and engaged in each of our lives if we will allow Him to participate. We all face difficulties in life, it is the reality of life. How we encounter them is our choice.

It must also be noted that when we do not control our focus, as in directed to the Lord Jesus Christ, we can bring forth grave problems into our lives. David took his focus away from God and placed it on the world when he looked at Bathsheba while she was bathing, "And from the roof he saw a woman bathing, and the woman was very beautiful to behold."[52] It was one thing to look but another to not look away. He made a decision to turn his vision from God and to focus his intent upon this woman – I am not being judgmental here, it is simply an operative decision that he

---

[52] 2Samuel 11:2.

made. The outcome saw death and destructive in his life and the life of others. *Focusing upon God and taking control over one's ability to focus is of God.* Choosing to focus upon things of the world brings forth loss of potential and fullness of life at the very least.

As a boy of 12 Jesus made a shift in reality, at least to a further degree and one that became more intensified. Isn't that the same with each of us? Each of us, you and me, have within us the seed of God's implanted presence and love.[53] The key here is that Jesus made a choice, the right choice to be who He was created to be and that is the Son of God. *Each of us is a son or daughter of God, if we will but awaken to that reality.* The Gospel of John speaks of those who accept Him in this way, "But as many as received Him, to them He gave the right to become children of God, to those who believe in His name."[54] Yes, you may find that a stretch just as Jesus' parents did when they found Jesus in the Temple. Remember it was there that Jesus first declared Himself the direct child of God

---

[53] Colossians 3:11b.
[54] John 1:12.

the Father.[55] What a statement of faith. You may say that for Jesus it was not a statement of faith because He was in fact the Son of God, however, He was also a twelve year old boy who was fully human. I believe this decision for Him was an awakening of His faith. *Faith, as it applies to God and His children, is the connecting awareness of ultimate relationship* – pure and simple. Faith is something which must be known and lived to be real and only true reality can display true faith.

Faith is both a verb and a noun. *Faith as a known reality without action is meaningless*[56]. So for you, me or anyone to gain a greater awareness of who we truly are we must come and act in faith – just as Jesus did as that 12 year old boy. To focus upon one's true source of strength one must believe in that source and rely upon that source. Focus and faith are directly interconnected. In fact one cannot exist without the other. *Faith brings*

---

[55] Jesus' declaration that He was in fact the living Son of God is one of the main reasons that He was crucified. There will be a clash in the world when we chose Jesus as our source of truth, yet it is our true path to fulfillment.
[56] See James 2:17.

one to proper focus and proper focus brings one into the fullness of faith[57]. Faith and focus can bring forth the presence of Jesus into our lives *in the here and now of our being* and that is the start of a new understanding of who you truly are, with new potential, new possibilities – not because of you, but because of Jesus who truly loves you and is within you and with you. Let's take a look at a life that is grounded in Jesus and how the power of focus can have a real effect.

Some years ago a pastor friend shared this true story with me and has allowed me to share it with others. It was a vibrate ministry and the reality of the Lord stirred in that faith family. One particular family that attended believed in centering their lives upon Jesus and staying focused upon Him. As they raised their young daughter through the years the father would nurture her in the principle of faith focus. He would tell her repeatedly over the years that whatever happens she was to "stand in the faith." If she was at a point of making a significant decision she was to "stand in the faith". If she was confronted by a problem, she was to "stand in the faith." She heard

---

[57] Colossians 3:1-2.

this over and over during her growing up years. One afternoon when she was twelve years old, as she got off the school bus, she joined her friends along the side of the road to talk for a few minutes. There she stood by the side of the road, with tall grass just a few feet away, intently engaged in her conversation. She noticed out of the corner of her eye a snake coming out from the grass headed directly towards her. She didn't have time to respond before the snake was at her feet. Naturally startled, she stood there for a moment not able to move. The snake was a rattlesnake and it proceeded to wrap itself around her leg. What was she to do? She did exactly what her father had taught her to do – she stood in the faith. I have to believe that she went immediately into prayer and the heavens were opened up before her.

Like Daniel in the Lion's Den, her focus was so intense that she was more present with God than with that snake. As she stood there, "standing in the faith" the rattlesnake unwrapped itself and went back into the grass. Like Daniel, this is the reality of the power of focus and each one of us decides each moment of our lives what we will focus upon. It is the willful power of decision that

God has granted to humanity. It is the one true human power that cannot be taken away and is our true human freedom that is the power of will to make a choice. It does take effort, intentionality and desire, yet as we see with Daniel and this young girl it provides a power that can overcome the hurtful and harmful powers of the world. **Focus, Empowered by Faith, is the Foundational Means to Receive the Power of Jesus**:

How you use your time and energy and where you direct it is essential to who you will be. Unlike many aspects of life, Jesus gives you a geometric return on your time and energy invested in Him. See Acts 2:25- 28 for how King David approached this understanding in life.

A Moment of Reflection:

What do you focus upon during your day? How do you spend your time? What TV shows do you watch or music do you listen to? Do you focus upon God by reading Scripture? Do you use meditation or prayer? Do you fellowship with those of like spirit? God gives you the freedom of will to make that decision – it's your choice; this is called being intentional.

Intentional Action:

I want to encourage you to go right now and read Psalm 121. Not just read it for the sake of reading, but read it and sit there with it, thinking about the words you have heard. Let the words become one with your spirit- read it until it becomes one with your heart. This might take place in one setting or over a period of days. David said, "I will lift up my eyes to the hills – from where will my help come?" David's eyes were totally focused upon the Lord at the writing of this psalm. I want to ask you to do something that may be new for you. Pray this psalm back to God. Pray it as if it were your own words. God won't object that you take these words into yourself until they become one with you, in fact He will delight in it. There are no more perfect words than God's and when we become one with them there is a reality of power in unity that edifies our hearts and spirits. You do not have to recite them word for word. Express the feeling in your own words, as you take the word of God into you and call out to God from your heart. This is a great psalm of encouragement and power. Whenever you intentionally focus upon God, in this case through His word, God will respond. Jesus is a 24/7 God, He never sleeps nor slumbers. Do as David did, lift your eyes to God in all situations.

Write Some of Your Thoughts:

Explore your feelings. As you read and take in these words from Psalm 121, what do you hear God saying to you? What do these words mean to your life? What in your life is God asking you to accept or change?

_____

_____

_____

_____

_____

_____

_____

_____

_____

_____

_____

_____

7

Swimming in the Stream of God's Grace in a World of Negativity

There is a stream that makes glad the city of God.[58]

As you start to realize your new potential you will also start to realize that you are not alone. You are no longer isolated from God and dependent upon what others think. *You will start to realize that in this reconstruction of your relationship with God there is an uplifting strength within you that is greater than yourself.* This happens the more you place your focus upon God and less upon yourself – it is a growing process of your new life. It is an eternal force of goodness in your life and you will start to feel increasingly better about yourself. As you leave behind the false understanding of who you are you can now start to realize the true you and realize the wonder of the riches you have within you.

---

[58] Psalm 46:4.

There are two basic streams of force in creation: one is belittling, destroying and life taking, the other is life giving, encouraging, uplifting and growing. Jesus recognized this reality when He said, "The thief does not come except to steal, and to kill, and to destroy. I have come that they may have life, and that they may have it more abundantly." [59] It is the goal of Jesus that you have a life of joy and abundance. Remember what Jesus said in John 15:11, "These things I have said, that My joy may remain in you and that your joy may be full." This true expression of the reality of life of abundance and joy comes out of Jesus' existence as the "presence of Truth" in one's life. Anyone who has lived beyond the age of innocence, being honest with themselves and truthful about the world around us, would concur with the understanding of Jesus. Why do people hurt others and not love, why instead of finding a common ground do nations go to war, why do people try to get richer than their neighbors and want to have power over their neighbors instead of blessing them with a gift of sharing? That is the reality of the world. That is why people in the world are still

---

[59] John 10:10.

starving, that is why the vast majority of people in the world don't have clean drinking water, that is why more money is spent on military in the world than on uplifting the hurting, that is why the prison industry (at least in the United States) is one of the fastest growing industries, and the list goes on. Yet, in the midst of all of this we are told that there is a river – a stream that flows with gladness. This stream is like a natural river as one would swim in, it engulfs you in its current and substance. It has direction and carries all who flow in it towards its ending point. In this stream one discovers the motion that is necessary to stay afloat, assisted by the natural nature of its buoyancy. This stream is the river of grace, created for God's children to carry them in their journey of life. Simply put, Jesus is with you and is willing to place His very Holy Spirit within you, to guide you, to teach you in truth and to comfort and protect you. Yet, there is more, as you are reinstated in your relationship with Jesus you will be enfolded in a present force of His living grace.

Isaiah speaks of this nature of the force of grace as a living reality (Isa. 35:8-9). He says it is "A highway" that "shall be there, and a road and it shall be called the Highway of Holiness." He goes on to tell us that those who don't have a real and active relationship with Jesus will not be able to walk on this highway but it will be for those who are restored to an active and present relationship with God through Jesus – "But the redeemed shall walk there." Isaiah says that the living presence of God's self will assist you on this path. Not even fools can get lost on this path because of the present force of Jesus' assisting grace. Maybe you are like me and really like that thought. Do you ever feel that you don't have it all together? Sometimes I think about how insufficient I am, but that's the point – God's grace is sufficient for us even in those times. All we have to do is to believe, yes, by faith, love Him in our hearts and He will see us through. It even gets richer. Isaiah says, "No lion shall be there, nor shall any ravenous beast go on it; it shall not be found there." In other words, all of those condemning words and people who still speak negative words towards you can NOT have any authority over you. You are in the privileged authority of God's present grace.

Gregory of Nyssa, a fourth century bishop of Nyssa, uses these words to describe this same reality, "For the river of grace flows everywhere; its source is not in Palestine, nor does it flow into the sea there, but encircles the whole earth and empties itself into paradise."[60] Gregory is stating that in the world with its negative and destructive force there is present a positive power and that power flows throughout the whole earth and has a present and eternal connection to the source of true life – which is the living grace of Jesus. This river or stream is one of grace and has its creation, truth and power in the very substance of Jesus Christ. Jesus Christ is the one true source of whole, restored and fulfilled life. Like Christy Brown, he was not whole as the world would expect, but once he found that stream of grace he became more and more fulfilled. This "river of grace" which Gregory speaks of is a present force of life. Like the force of gravity it is real yet cannot be seen in material form but its results can be realized. It is a force, like gravity, and it has its effects upon those who understand it and honor it. If one struggles against

---

[60] John E. Rotelle, ed., *Tradition, Day by Day: Readings from Church Writers* (Villanova, PA: Augustinian Press, 1994), 259.

the force of gravity they become defeated, for it is a force too great for the individual to overcome. Grace is also a profound force in life, but unlike gravity which is meant to hold us down physically on the earth, grace is meant to lift us up in spirit and joy, and to encourage us along the way of life. The key to this path of power is Jesus.

Even if one does not realize the nature or power of grace and the reality of Jesus Christ as its source, one can still benefit from its blessing. However the ones who benefit the most are those that recognize its reality and are in harmony with its presence and current flow of power. Like those soldiers of the Army of Constantine walking through that cave, the ones who were most open to the present riches were most blessed! They took advantage of what was present even though they could not see its immediate reality – that is a form of faith. The message here is to be open and watch the wonder of what happens in your life – as Apostle Paul says in his first letter to the Corinthians 15:43, speaking of the ones who are connected to the reality of the grace of the living Jesus, they are "raised in power." The reforming power of grace will take you from the negative force of the world into the positive power of Jesus. It will allow you to understand your true infinite worth that is the shared glory of God's self through Jesus.

Let me share with you a most wondrous true story. It comes to us by way of the Gospel of John. Jesus was coming of age in His spiritual maturity and setting out in ministry. He had gathered disciples to walk with Him and to learn from Him. He and His disciples were invited to a wedding at Cana of Galilee. From the telling of the story, for the most part they stayed in the background, in the area where the servants were and where all of the preparations for the feast were taking place.

In the culture of that time, this event was a major happening for the community. Family, relatives and dear friends would have come from miles around and from distance villages. This event would have lasted as long as a week and maybe even longer. It was filled with great expectation. As things were coming together and the feast was in its beginning stages, there became a shortage of wine. As wine was the main source of festive drink this had the potential of ruining the celebration. It would have come to an abrupt halt. Because it was the responsibility of the bridal families to provide for their guests this would have been a sign of contempt and lack of caring. It could have easily ended in strife and hostility.

The dye was cast for disappointment, failure and broken relationship. All of this was true – the world in and of itself cannot offer fulfillment of life. It will always fall short and there will be pain, hurt and sorrow except for one factor. That one exception is the presence of Jesus. Where Jesus is there is potential for complete and fulfilled life. Jesus is not only the God of *new beginnings* but the God of *true life*.

It is interesting to note that Jesus' mother Mary, upon discovering that the wine had in fact run out, went immediately to Jesus because she knew He had the power to change the course of events. He responded to her, "My hour has not yet come." Then she said to the servants, "Whatever He says to you, do it." Mary not only knew the power of Jesus, but she acknowledged the supremacy of His will and acquiesced to Jesus and His authority in that moment of need. It was out of her *knowledge and reality of her need* that she found the strength to accept the power of Jesus over the situation. So often people go through life in denial, covering over their real need and never fulfilling that need – the one essential human need for fulfillment is Jesus Christ in the heart of the believer. Are you truly aware of the lack of fulfillment in your life and the need for change?

Though Jesus' hour had not yet come, He reacted out of His true nature of love and compassion. He knew the festivity would come to a disastrous close if He didn't do something positive in that situation. He also knew He was the only one able to correct the situation. He, out of His true nature of grace and love, changed the course of all eternity for the benefit of that couple and for all humanity. By His action of sending the servants to fill the water pots with water and changing the water into wine, not just any wine, but the very finest wine in all of creation, He caused renewal of celebration of life for that wedding and for all of humanity. I say all of humanity because when we find Jesus in our midst – yes, His very presence, then we can have the fulfillment of the meaning of life. We also find that He is the one who changes the dullness of our lives from bland to spectacular, from ordinary to exceptional and from the stagnant waters of life into the flow of the stream of grace which is the wine He has created for your life.

For us to receive the full meaning of this event that Jesus uses as a teaching, we must understand what Mary did. She came to a point of her own understanding to know her limitations and to realize that Jesus and Jesus alone was the *power of change* in that circumstance. It is when we, as children of God, come to the reality that we all have a need that only Jesus can supply that it takes proper direction and focus. It would have done Mary no good at all to have gone to the head steward and told him of the need. He didn't have the power to effect a change in the outcome of the event. *As God's children we must first discover our real need before our real want is fulfilled. Our real need in any situation is to be present with Jesus at all times. He is the only one who will speak truth into our hearts and give us this wondrous wine of fulfillment.*

When we discover our real need and go to the true source that has the power to change the situation, then our lives will begin to change in a constructive way and we begin to flow in the realm of grace which Gregory tells us about. That realm of grace, just like a river, will engulf you and give you buoyancy throughout your life's journey and carry you all the way into eternal paradise. It will act as your guide for direction as you flow in its current and by its force it will protect you. It is a force for life and life more abundant. As we journey in this stream of grace we find that our movement to reach harmony with its current is essential. In this way we maximize the benefits of its ability to carry us forward with the least amount of discomfort and stress. It is learning to be in harmony with the will of Jesus for our lives. This river is Jesus' assisting presence with you. It is His living grace which is His gift for you.

This stream of grace also gives us the present feeling of its strength about us to uplift us and to support us in all circumstances. Like Mary, all we have to do is to ask. Jesus tells us and shows us that there is nothing that will stand between us and His love for us (see Romans 8:35- 39), except for maybe our pride – being too self-proud to ask Jesus for help. He has never in all of the days of creation turned down anyone who has called out to Him and said, "Jesus, come into my heart and be my light of life."

Jesus Calls You to be Intentional:

His relationship with you is the most important thing to the heart of God, if you need a witness of that reality look to the Cross of Jesus. Jesus wants you to know that you are His – that should be the definition of who you are. He also wants you to be in a living and love filled relationship with Him, in other words to have a passion for Him as He has a passion for you. Definition and passion are essential, however they are only put into motion by your level of intentional action – you simply must engage to receive the greatest benefit.

A Moment of Reflection:

Take the time to read the second chapter of the Gospel of John, verses 1-11 and think about the reality of the story and how it might relate to your life. Is your life one of celebration and one that has real substance so that it can continue or is it about to run out of energy? Maybe things are going well, but what happens when things change and don't go so well? What happens if you don't' get the promotion you were expecting, or even worse, lose your job? What happens if the stock market crashes again and your savings are depleted? Do you know the one who can help you in those times of crises? The truth of life is that we need real substance under the surface of our smiles, under the surface of our patterns of life to coincide with our daily expectations. It is not just words that the culture will use to make us feel less than adequate, it can be situations. All negative forces lend to a distorted understanding of our worth – our esteem. Like the couple at that wedding at Cana, Jesus is able to show you that you are eternally special in His created order! Think about that for a moment.

Maybe you are like Mary, the mother of Jesus, and you are certain beyond all doubt that Jesus is the source of true happiness and joy. Yet, even Mary had to come to the point of giving up control in her life, of turning the control of her life over to Jesus – that takes strength. It takes a sense of reality in truth to focus upon the One who can supply all of our heartfelt needs. It calls for a shift from being self-centered to being *Jesus-focused*. Just as Jesus is primarily focused upon the Heavenly Father, so we must be primarily focused upon Jesus – *focus is essential.* Whether in words or actions, when we accept negative spiritual flow into our being it shifts our focus away from the force of creation to the force of destruction and decay.

Maybe you are like the servants, you have seen what Jesus can do in the life of others but you have not made it your intention to follow Him and make that shift real in the course of your life? Let me ask you, isn't it time to leave the hurt of the world behind, to come to a place of new possibilities just as Jesus offered that couple at the wedding? You simply need to drink of what it is that Jesus is offering you. Isn't it time to let go and give in to Him wholly and completely? You know how to do that, simply stop right now and say to Jesus – "Now is the time I need You, help me to open up to You and fill me with Your love and grace, please Jesus, I need you now." He will not disappoint you.

Maybe you are like the bride and groom and the master of the feast, you see good things that have happened in your life in the past but don't give the acknowledgement to the one true source of that reality. This is the reality that John Newton wrote about in his famous song, *Amazing Grace*. Throughout John's life good things happened when he didn't deserve them and even when bad things happened he somehow had the strength to survive. It wasn't until late in his life that he realized it was Jesus who had been with him through it all. This caused him to fall to his knees in the wonder of it all and to thank Jesus with the words of his song.

Hopefully, you are like the disciples who understood Jesus as a teacher, and then saw what He did at the wedding and "believed in Him."[61] It was the disciples who left that wedding with a total new sense of reality and attitude of who they were and the new potential of what life could and would offer. Coupled into the power of the presence of Jesus they knew that their lives were entering a *realm of new beginnings and great possibilities.* That is that stream of grace that Gregory of Nyssa

---

[61] John 2:11.

talks about. It is a living force of the presence of Jesus upon your life.

This is a time to search your heart. Be honest with yourself and understand your true need in life. It is a time to develop the want for the One who can give you fulfilled life and abundant joy – like the wine Jesus made, it is infinite in its goodness and infinite in its supply. You have nothing to lose by asking Jesus to be the one in your life to give you that new meaning – that new attitude – it is so easy and so present for you. No matter where you are in your journey of life, if you are just getting to know Jesus or if you are a seasoned disciple – the key to growth in God-esteem which is your true value comes through giving up control to Jesus. Jesus is the new wine. He is that positive force that will replace the old and bruised image that the world has created in you with joy and great expectation, yes, even with the happiness of who you are – since you are that very finest wine.

Intentional Action:

During your daily routines I want to ask you to go to Jesus in prayer – in the little things and the great needs. Exercise your strength to focus first upon Him and call out to Him in the inner part of your being, that place of your heart and soul. In this way you will place Jesus first and foremost in your mind. It takes being intentional in your life, but the reward is great power in Jesus and being filled with joy *Now* and forever!

Write Your Thoughts:

As you write some thoughts be honest with yourself. Are you willing or have you released control of your life over to Jesus? Are there times that you keep taking control back from Jesus? Where are you now in this process?

_____

_____

_____

_____

_____

_____

_____

_____

_____

_____

8

Learning to Listen to the Correct Voices

"But we have this treasure in earthen vessels, that the excellence of the power may be of God and not of us" [62]

As you grow in your new understanding of your true worth – *God-worth*, the God within you, you should begin to discern the difference between words spoken to you that are godly and those that are ungodly. The more you grow closer to Christ Jesus and the *reality* that He is one with you, the easier it will be for you to know when someone is speaking untruth to you. James, the brother of Jesus, directs us to the importance of what we speak, "So then, my beloved brethren, let every person be swift to hear, slow to speak, slow to

---

[62] 2 Corinthians 4:7.

wrath".[63] What James is encouraging us to do is to process what we think and say through the truth of Jesus. When one is baptized into the Christian faith they become united into the reality and existence of God by the power of the Holy Spirit and the power of God's grace (as we discussed in the last chapter) and start to take upon themselves the characteristics of Jesus – if they are staying focused. In that state of renewal they will *experience* what is known as the fruit of the Spirit. The fruit of the Spirit, as told to us in Galatians 5:25, is love, peace, joy, faithfulness, patience, self-control, gentleness, kindness, and generosity. As one accepts the way and truth of Jesus into their hearts and minds then they grow in the way of the Spirit of God within themselves and exhibit gentleness, kindness and generosity towards each other. This is what James is referring to; *that a true spirit of love towards others is uplifting and edifying of one's own spirit.* Conversely, words that are not of God are destructive, hurtful and oppressive of one's own being. The choice is always ours! This is what we discussed in the last chapter, that there are two forces in the world, one of

---

[63] James 1:19.

destruction and one of creation. So what James is encouraging is that we should be careful of the words we use and recognize the difference between words that are of godliness and the words that are ungodly, words that will uplift and encourage and the words that defeat and destroy.

James goes on to declare that the tongue is one of the most powerful muscles within the human body. Hear what he says, "Look also at ships: although they are so large and are driven by fierce winds, they are turned by a very small rudder wherever the pilot desires. Even so the tongue is a little member and boasts great things. See how great a forest a little fire kindles!"[64] What is in the heart will eventually come out of the mouth. Listen to what Jesus says in Luke 6:45, "A good man out of the good treasure of his heart brings forth good; and an evil man out of the evil treasure of his heart brings forth evil. For out of the abundance of the heart his mouth speaks." The word comes out of the mouth and has the ability to create or destroy. In this way as you grow in your understanding of your true God-worth, you will have the ability to be a creating force as God is a creating force. In this

Learning to Listen to the Correct Voices

---

[64] James 3:4-5.

manner you and I become co-creators with God for healing and good in this world. That is an awesome reality, is it not?

It is essential that if we are going to live our lives to the fullest we need to let God enter our hearts and let God direct our thoughts and speech. It is also necessary that we recognize this principle in the conversation with others. Are they speaking words of truth, words of gentleness and kindness in a spirit of generosity? Are we hoping to do for them the goodness that God has done for us?

There is another aspect of the 'fruit of the Spirit'[65] Once you accept Christ into your heart the Holy Spirit pours the love of God into your heart as a free gift of grace. This is given to you out of the unlimited love that God has for you.[66] This is God's free gift of grace for you. This love of God poured out into our hearts gives us the sense within us of 'living hope'. As Apostle Paul tells us in Romans 5:5, this "hope does not disappoint." In other words, our hearts and spirits are always uplifted by God's participating presence within us – the in pouring of

---

[65] If you are not aware of the 'fruit of the Spirit' as a gift given to you by God then please read Galatians 5:22-23. Galatians 5:1-26 will give you a more complete picture.
[66] Romans 5:5.

God's love into our hearts is God speaking the Word of Truth into our hearts. Here we come back to the principle of faith. If by faith we accept that this wondrous gift is within us then we will feel that uplifting. This will help us discern the words that are spoken to us. *If they uplift or edify us in the greater image of God then it is likely that the words are of God.* If they are said in love, gentleness, kindness and a spirit of generosity then it is likely that they are godly in nature.[67] As James tells us, we must be "swift to hear", think about what is being said to you by another person or through the media that you are listening to, does it fit the truth of Jesus, is it what Jesus would say to you? Is what is being said to you of God or not? Is it something that you want to take ownership of or discard? Here it is extremely helpful to know the word of

---

[67] Whether a person speaks to you in a Godly Spirit or a worldly spirit, it is essential that you apply discernment to each instance. A person may be well intended, yes, even one grounded in Jesus, but they may not be speaking for God at that moment. The burden of responsibility is with the hearer. If you are struggling with discernment concerning a specific issue or comment made to you, take it to a fellowship of Christians or your pastor for guidance. Always verify it over and against the love, truth and grace of Jesus Christ.

God through Scripture which helps you validate the truth of the spoken word. These are active decisions that are made throughout each day. If you don't use this method to evaluate what is being said to you, you will in fact open yourself up to anything that is said and receive untruth and hurtful understandings that can be very harmful to you and your personal growth. *The act of not participating in the power that God offers you is to place yourself under the false will of others.* You must be in control of yourself in any situation, in other words, use the authority that God has given you. Ultimately, each of us will accept a truth, either God's truth or a false understanding as a truth.

Each of us has authority to accept or reject what comes into our being. Each of us must test what is said against the truth of God which is revealed in God's word of revelation. Therefore it is important that you spend time reading God's word – Scripture. It really is a joyful experience and will uplift you and create in you a new heart and a strong spirit.[68] Through this living interaction with

---

[68] Psalm 51:10, see also Psalm 119:15-16.

God's word you will realize how amazingly wonderful God's love for you truly is. Let's again take Psalm 121 for an example: "I will lift up mine eyes to the hills – from whence come my help? My help comes from the LORD, who made heaven and earth. He will not allow your foot to be moved; He who keeps you will not slumber. Behold, He who keeps Israel shall neither slumber nor sleep. The LORD is your keeper; The LORD is your shade at your right hand. The sun shall not strike you by day, Nor the moon by night. The LORD shall preserve you from all evil; He shall preserve your soul. The LORD shall preserve your going out and your coming in From this time forth, and even forevermore."

Here we see that God is with us always, in good times and bad. It is God who never leaves us but is there to protect us and enhance our lives. He keeps us within His heart of love and with His power of grace that enfolds the lives of those who are willing to walk with Him. "I look up to the hills – from whence comes my help?" states the reality that life is full of challenges and some of these challenges can potentially be very destructive, however, the psalmist immediately responses that there is a power far greater than the world and that power is with you. Just by reading those words and taking them into your heart as your living reality it will give you strength beyond any measure. Only the One who has the power to impact your heart and spirit in such a manner is the Lord Jesus Christ. Think about it, we are made in such a manner that no one has the ability to get into our hearts and souls if we do not allow them. It is all based upon the *principle of will*. God has given each of us the basic power of will – the ability to make willful decisions, to allow and disallow things to enter our inner-being. It is the will to grow in the truth of the creating God that enhances our lives to the level of this prophet who found such courage, strength and direction from this new reality; not a false reality as spoken to you by many, but a true reality spoken to you in love and hope, "For I know the thoughts that I think of you, says the Lord, thoughts of peace and not of evil, to give you a future and a hope. Then you will call on Me and go and pray to Me, and I will listen to you. And you will seek Me and find Me, when you search for Me with all your heart"[69]

---

[69] Jeremiah 29:11.

Jesus is there to assist us in making these willful decisions if we give Him the opportunity. As the words above tell us, He wants the very best for us but we must be willing to participate with Him and be active in that process. This is what the wonder of grace is about, the one true God who is Jesus Christ, helping us along the way. Yes, Jesus is there to help you in making your willful decisions if you will but seek Him and ask Him, either by prayer or inward reflection. We are told in Ephesians 2:8-9 this beautiful truth, "For by grace you have been saved through faith, and that not of you; it is a gift from God, not of works, lest anyone should boast. For we are His workmanship, created in Christ Jesus for good works, which God prepared beforehand that we should walk in them." The good news is that Jesus is the living God who is with us to help us, guide us, comfort us and strengthen us in our way of life.

Within You is the True Treasure of Life Itself:

The living presence of Jesus, where He and the Holy Spirit dwell are the treasure within you. This is your true worth: God-worth and no one in all of creation can change that with any words or any action. It is your God-given gift – the treasure in your earthen vessel. See John 14:12-21 and 15:1-5.

A Moment of Reflection:

Now that you have realized that you are the living specialness of God and that you are never alone, for He is there always to assist you and to guide you, you will have the strength of God to follow His path for your life and not be blown about by the winds of this world. This is the essence of the *Principle of God-worth*, that you are more than you!!! Think about that. My name is Gordon and that is who I am in this world, especially to others, but by knowing the reality of Jesus who dwells within me (see Ephesians 2:19 – 22), then I become Gordon plus the living presence of the Lord. I am, in effect, more than myself – a whole lot more. The same is true for you. You may have to pause for a moment here and say to yourself, "I am going to accept this by faith in Jesus Christ and in Him alone.", because what I am offering you can only be realized by faith in Jesus and the more complete your faith the more realized this reality will become for you. Once that bridge is crossed a wondrous new world opens up for you and you will have strength that you never realized before.

Intentional Action:

I want to encourage you to say to yourself, using your name, "I am _____(your name)____ plus the Lord Jesus within me. I am the living temple of the indwelling God."[70] That is the truth! Once you come to the fullness of that reality you will have "living joy" that no one can take away. That is in fact the real definition of joy – the "realized presence of Jesus within you."[71] Jesus tells us in Hebrews 13:5, "I will never leave you nor forsake you."

Again, I want to encourage you through the next few days and maybe weeks to bring this point to mind as you go about your daily routine. As you stop and pause during the day, focus upon the Lord in this living reality, maybe include this reality into your prayer life. This is the intimacy that Jesus wants to have with you.

---

[70] 1 Corinthians 6:19.
[71] This topic of the true definition of joy is covered in my book, *"Seeing Through the Eyes of Heaven: An Encounter with God"*.

Write Some of Your Thoughts:

How does this concept settle in your inner being? How do you feel about this? Are you accepting its full worth? How does it feel to know that you are more than you ever realized since you are you + Jesus Christ within you?

_____

_____

_____

_____

_____

_____

_____

_____

_____

9

The Real You –
Grounded in the Truth of
God

"Create in me a clean heart, O God, and renew a steadfast spirit within me."[72]

Once you read Scripture and fellowship with those of like-spirit you will continue to grown stronger in the Spirit of God and God's way through the likeness of Jesus Christ. As a pastor I see this transition take place constantly and it is beautiful. The metaphor of a caterpillar going through the stages of metamorphosis becomes a reality in the life of those who give in to the will of Christ Jesus. This rather ruff looking creature called a caterpillar transforms into a creature that is no longer earth bound, but can take flight and soar over the earth and not only that, but is spectacular in its magnificence. That wonder is within you waiting to be lived out! Henri Nouwen said in his book, "The

---

[72] Psalm 51:10.

Life of the Beloved", that what Christians have the hardest time accomplishing is to simply accept that they truly are the *beloved* of Christ Jesus.[73] Again, by faith we accept this and then the transformation starts to work. *Faith is the catalyst in this process.*

Also, as a pastor, I see those who don't commit themselves wholly to the process of belief by faith and they struggle or stagnate. They don't grow and reach the joy that is waiting for them. For sure there are times of struggle and challenge and it is not all bliss, but the certainty comes out of a strong faith commitment to accept the truth of God even through the struggles of life. God will use the struggles and obstacles to strengthen your faith and to teach you, even grow you in His way. Remember, "For God so loved the world"[74]and God "so loves" you, yes, even more than God's self. Jesus in all of His glory will never leave you nor forsake you, but will eternally be with you to guide you and assist you.[75]

Once I was driving along the Great Smoky Mountain Ridge with a friend when we saw this

---

[73] Henri Nouwen, *Life of the Beloved* (New York: Crossroad Publishing), 30.
[74] John 3:16.
[75] John 14:26 and Hebrews 13:5.

group of people gathered at this observation point and I turned the car into that area. As we entered the area this man approached the car with a great level of excitement. My friend and I were still in the car and couldn't understand what was happening. As we got out of the car this man told us that they had been waiting there for two weeks and finally it was happening, well, we still didn't know what he was talking about, but he got our interest. Then he said that the migration of the Monarch butterflies was in process and they annually come down through that valley. As we watched we could see the butterflies coming up out of the valley, landing on the plants and flowers to rest and feed. Then something spectacular happened, we were approximately 4,000 feet high and the mountain edge cut shapely down into a valley that deep. The butterflies would launch out into the air over that 4,000 foot valley and soar upon the wind currents. It was the highest mountain in the area and as they took flight there was no 'next stop' for miles, only air to fly into at amazing heights. Think of it – it is all but impossible, this little butterfly that doesn't even weigh an ounce and is now piloting through the air in magnificent wonder. They were not flying by their strength because the reality is that they had no strength. The trees below standing 40 to 60' high had strength to stand against the elements and the rocks and boulders were strong enough to weather the storms for centuries but what strength did these little weightless wonders have? It is such a wonder because it defines all practical physical possibilities. No fear, no doubt, there they launched just being carried by the knowledge that it can be done because there is a greater force than what is visible to the human eye – that is faith and its manifestation. They were doing what they had been created to do. You have been created to soar in the Spirit of God – yes, to

be lifted up and carried by His strength and to feel the wonder of the hands of Jesus carrying you to new heights of joy and living reality of His unity with you.

Knowing and accepting that you are the beloved and that you are favored in the heart of God is the ultimate empowering agent of the principle of faith. This is when you will have the strength to believe God's truth for you over the defeating words and actions of the oppressors of life. I don't think that the caterpillar, in its un-transformed state, has any idea that it will one day soar to great heights with such marvel. In fact, I don't think it even thinks about it, but it simply does what it has been created to do – just as you need to do, you have been created to soar in the likeness of the perfect loving God!

There stood an eight year old boy, baseball glove in hand, in the middle of human poverty where hope looked like an alien object. His father was a baseball player but was out of the country most of the time playing the game he loved. This boy had a dream, like his father, it was to become a great baseball player. Living in the Dominican Republic where poverty was a normal state, he held onto his dream as only a child could – hoping against all the odds in the reality of a fallen and impoverished world. Like Jesus this twelve year old boy had a vision, a greater identity within him than the world offered and wasn't going to let it be denied. One has to wonder how many times voices spoke to this young boy and said, "You best get real and find a job." and "Stop chasing rainbows." In the midst of the poverty of spirit in this world he focused upon a power within and was willing to believe that power.

At the age of sixteen he immigrated to the United States where he started playing baseball during his high school years in Kansas City. He was an outstanding player, hitting 22 homeruns one season – what potential! He knew who he was and he knew his true source of strength. However, when he made a decision to submit his name for the 1999 major league draft he was met with rejection. Like Jesus shows us – the world often responds in words of disbelief and condemnation. 401 players were selected before him and it wasn't until the 13th round that his name was finally selected – and then only for a minor team in the minor league. He said he was hurt to the point of tears – rejection is painful! Rejection comes in many forms –not just words, but circumstances. He worked through the pain, remembering who he was and who was standing with him and accepted the opportunity to play for that minor league team. We, as children of God must shift our focus from false teachings to righteous teachings. Often life doesn't look pretty along the way, but if we stay focused and faithful to the One who can provide,

He will deliver us to His fulfilled purpose in our lives.

In the minor league he demonstrated outstanding baseball skills and after one season he was brought into the major league to play for the Kansas City Chiefs. You may already know him, his name is Albert Pujols. In his first ten seasons as a major league player he never hit below a .300 batting average, he never hit less than 30 homeruns and never had less than 100 runs batted in.

As a child and through his formative years he could have given in to the reality of the poverty of his environment, the voices of the major league draft selectors which said he didn't quite have what it takes but he choose to listen to a far greater voice who said, "It is I who have created you and I know the plans I have for you, plans for a future with hope."[76] Albert Pujols says this of his family and their focus in life, "In the Pujols' family, God is first. Everything else is a distant second."[77]

---

[76] Jeremiah 29:11.
[77] Wikipedia. Albert Pujols, en.wikipedia.org/wiki/Pojols (accessed March 24, 2014).

When Jesus says that we should love our Heavenly Father with all of our heart, mind, soul and strength, He is saying this because it is the true focus and source of our joy in life. Jesus wants us to have and experience the best – that inner sense of who we truly are, not as the world tells us but as God Almighty has spoken into us through His Son, Jesus Christ. In 2011 Albert Pujols joined his team in capturing the World Series championship. All of this because he didn't let the voices of the world dictate to him his true potential. He made a shift away from the false voices to the one true voice of life – Jesus, the one who wants you to "have life and to have it more abundantly."[78]

For focus to be accomplished you must simply accept the possibility that you too are a son or daughter of God, the Most High. You have a direct and present, 24/7 connection to Jesus, who is your living God. Jesus said as He walked with His disciples, "While you have the light, believe in the

---

[78] John 10:10.

light, that you may become children of light."[79] I want you to stop here for a moment and think what it might be like to be the true son or daughter of God as Jesus has shown us? How would the acceptance of that reality change your life? Would you be like that 17 year old boy, able to heal from all of the crushing blows that life had dealt him? Would you be like Christy Brown, released into a wonder of *exceedingly great potential*? Would you be like Albert Pujols, staying strong through it all, the successes and failures, to ultimately be fulfilled in your humanity? If you say, "I can't do it!" You are correct! You cannot do it by yourself – but you can do it with the power of Jesus within you if you are willing to focus upon Him. Listen to these words from the Letter to the Ephesians 3:20, "Now to Him who is able to do exceedingly abundantly above all that we ask or think, according to the power that works in us." This is your relationship with Jesus, the power that works in you and He (Jesus) will do exceedingly abundantly above all that we ask or think! Isn't it time to join in this wondrous joy of

---

[79] John 12:36, here the NKJ translates "sons of light". I have used the NRSV translation in this instance, as it is properly more inclusive.

life and let yourself experience the love and power that Jesus wants you to know.

Jesus is an Assisting God:

He is already doing a good work in you. At this point in this exercise of learning you hopefully have already made great strides forward. Keep directing yourself in a positive spirit. Once you realize this unity you have with Jesus within you, you become a creating positive force for Him in creation. Suggested reading, John 21, especially read verses 15- 17.

A Moment of Reflection:

Once you realize the truth of the power of Jesus within you then you can unite with that living potential and reach the fullness of your true humanity – just remember, it's a life long journey. It may not be like Albert Pujols, hitting home runs before thousands of people, but it may be that you will find that wondrous peace in your spirit and be thankful for who you have been created to be – the beloved of God. If you reflect back on the teaching in chapter 7 about the stream of grace in creation, it is then that we feel the pressure taken off our shoulders. It is then that we realize it is all God's work, yes, by faith. We must be willing to let go and take that step of faith in God. Just like learning to swim, at some point we must release ourselves into the buoyancy of the water and take our feet off the ground. Once that happens, what a great and wondrous feeling it is – like learning to swim, flowing in God's will is a matter of letting go and giving in!

Intentional Action:

As you go forward from here I want to encourage you to keep in your mind and heart the understanding that Jesus swells within you and through Him you are infinitely connected through-out creation by His stream of grace. I am going to ask you to listen and watch for the movement of the Lord in your life. Jesus is going to be speaking to you, maybe through someone, through Bible readings, or devotions, or maybe that understanding that is deposited into your awareness, but He will be speaking to you. Watch for His presence in circumstances, through experiences, readings, meditations or reflections. Thomas a`Kempis, a Christian from the 15th century, said that in one moment of being enlightened by God our humble minds will comprehend more of eternal truth than could be learned by ten years in school.[80] Listening for the truth of God must be an intentional act and it will bear great fruit in our lives.

Write Some of Your Thoughts:

Have you experienced the presence of Jesus with you? Have you heard Him speak to you recently? When you pray do you take time to listen? If this is new to you, try writing down what ways you might be seeing Jesus' grace and presence with you – it could be something as simple as taking in the wonder of a beautiful flower or painting. By acknowledging it, you will start to train your spiritual senses to perceive this reality in your life.

_____

_____

_____

_____

_____

_____

_____

[80] Thomas a`Kempis, *The Imitation of Christ* (Mineloa, New York: Dover Publications), 91.

10

The Road Ahead

"These things I have spoken to you, that in Me you may have peace. In the world you will have tribulation; but be of good cheer, I have overcome the world."[81]

Now you know who you really are. You are created by God in His image to share the likeness of Jesus Christ. You know that you have the indwelling of God within you, that your body is the temple of this indwelling presence of the living God. The practical reality of this indwelling is that the very Spirit of God, the Holy Spirit, is within you to guide you, comfort you and teach you in the way of God. Not only are you not alone but *you are wonderfully enhanced by the living reality of God's self.* You have the force of the grace of Jesus with you, in you and about you to protect you, to provide for your way in life and to direct your path; remember John 14:20, "At that day you will know that I am in the Father, you in Me, and I in you."

---

[81] John 16:33.

You no longer stand alone but you stand with the eternal living strength of Jesus Christ. You no longer have self-worth, you now have God-worth and your self-esteem is replaced with God-esteem!

You know that your worth comes from the infinite love that God has for you and that He has practically empowered you to know that love and strength within you. God-worth is everything that is needed for a healthy and prosperous life. With God-worth within you there is nothing that can distort your sense of victory.

In the Gospel of Matthew we are told of two houses that are built, one was built upon rock and, "the floods came, and the winds blew and beat on that house; and it did not fall, for it was founded on the rock."[82] This is a clear metaphor for your new life, to know with all certainty that Jesus is your rock and foundation of life and if your foundation of life then your worth and your identity. Self is no longer sufficient, for you have shifted to a greater knowledge and reality. You have a higher level of consciousness. You now know who you are and whose you are – you are God's and God is yours. Self-esteem is a thing of

---

[82] Matthew 7:24–29.

the past and *God-esteem* is your new identity. Your sense of worth or esteem within you is now a joint-venture between your inner-being and the presence of Jesus with you in that inner place.

We are also told in the same passage that those that have this new found God-esteem within them will stand on the rock, but the ones who rely upon the self-esteem created by the world will fall, "But everyone who hears these sayings of Mine, and does not do them, will be like a foolish man who built his house on the sand: and the rain descended, the floods came, 'and the winds blew and beat on that house; and it fell. And great was its fall.'"

God-worth gives way to God-esteem and that is a realized reality of united power in Jesus Christ and you have awakened into this reality. God-esteem is the realized awareness that Jesus Himself is united with your spirit within you. In that way, when you are looking to your real strength you are not looking to self but to the unity of Jesus Christ within you. That is the basis of having living peace within you.[83] This is the teaching of Jesus Himself so that you will have the practical application of worth to give you success in your journey of life. Give this some thought – Did Jesus have self-esteem or God-esteem? The answer is certain – God-esteem. His total awareness is God-centered! So yours should be Jesus-centered, who is the revealed presence of God for His children. Look to Him, wait upon Him and follow Him and you, as the prophet Isaiah says, will be lifted up on wings like eagles and you will be renewed in strength, you will run and not be weary and you will walk and not stumble.[84] Like those monarch butterflies soaring over the valleys of the Great Smoky Mountains, you will soar to new heights in your inner-person, in relationships and in life.

Let me share with you an episode that just happened in my life this previous week as I was

---

[83] This is part of what takes place in the process of baptism. The Spirit of the living God comes and joins with your spirit and strengthens you in your inner-being. This coupling of the Holy Spirit of God with your spirit is what gives you superhuman strength, yet this is a potential and must be appreciated and exercised in order to receive the benefits.
[84] Isaiah 40:31.

working on this writing. I serve a small country church in Jennings, Fl. as a United Methodist pastor. This past Sunday the church family had arranged for a gospel music group to come and sing. They had been at our church the previous year and were wonderful in all ways. Everyone was looking forward to this event. The other churches in the area were invited. We were to listen to the gospel music and then have dinner in the fellowship hall. This all was to start at 4 P.M. My wife and I were running late and got there just a few minutes before 4 o'clock. As we entered the kitchen to drop off the food we had prepared it seemed strangely quiet. I walked down the hallway to the sanctuary and as I entered the sanctuary I saw the folks gathered, some from our church family and others from the local churches, it was a good gathering. However, as I looked around there was no gospel group – that's right, the group that we had all anticipated was not there. I went into my office and found one of the ladies of the church looking out the back window hoping for the group's bus to appear. It was an awkward situation to say the least. What to do? Everyone had gathered there with great expectation of a wonderful evening of music by this particular group. I could have looked to my own strength, felt defeated and sent everyone home in disappointment. However, there is far more to me than my own strength. I looked to the Jesus within me and walked out in front of all those people and greeted them in the Name and living presence of our Lord. I acknowledged that there was no singing group with us at the moment but told them that we always know that we are in the mist of Jesus' plan and movement in our lives. We came to prayer and gave thanksgiving for the Lord bringing us together and that we were waiting upon Him.

After finishing the prayer one of the lay leaders came to me and said that she was going to show a short video, the song on the video was "Amazing Grace". Then the phone rang – it was the gospel group. They said that they were in Tampa, Fl. which is four hours from our church. Somehow the wires got crossed and they weren't going to be there. I told this to those gathered and reminded them that our faith is in Jesus who has authority over all things and we are present in His grace. As I finished we watched the video, then a leader in the church got up and led us in some gospel songs, then two women got up and sang solos with amazingly beautiful voices. Meanwhile the Lord had laid a message and Scripture passage upon my heart (John 14:20) and I shared this with those gathered. It was a message on Christian unity. Then a call went out for all choir members to come forward and they sang, "Thank You for Giving to the Lord". After that we all went to the Fellowship Hall for our meal and it was a feast. We had more food than we could eat and we sent those who were in need home with their next day's dinner. All of this happened this way because we did not relay on our own strength but the power of Jesus within us – our God-esteem!

This is the living practicality of the shift to this new reality. It is real. It is abundant and it is life giving. In this you come into the power of God who through you creates in a wondrous way when the world fails.

God-esteem Gives You the Full Sense of Your True Worth:

This is based upon the love and strength of Jesus within you. When you realize that your spirit is united to the Spirit of God within you, your awareness becomes one of heavenly dimension. It is then that you increasingly lean upon the strength of Jesus for your true strength. It is in this way that you realize you are worth far more than 'self'- you are in fact – God enhanced to be God inspired! See the story of Gideon, Judges 6:34 – 7:23.

A Moment of Reflection:

In the American culture it is common that when meeting people you will be greeted with the phase, "How are you today?" Every time I hear that it brings me to the understanding of my God-esteem. If I truly understand that the Spirit of Jesus is united with my inner spirit then how can I be anything but joyous? If Jesus is with me, especially in such a wonderful and present way then in any circumstance I must admit that I am filled with joy. Since Jesus has defeated death, overcome all sin and evil and this presence of victory of life is within me then there isn't anything that I can't face or accomplish if it is called by the will of God. Think about this and how you now understand who you truly are.

Intentional Action:

As people greet you and ask you, "How are you?" before you respond think about who you truly are. Are you looking to the wonder of the source within you? It may give you an opportunity to witness to that person, that "Yes, I am filled with joy!" and ask them how they are? Most people are operating at low levels of their sense of worth and this can give you an opportunity to bless them, maybe offer them a copy of this writing. Maybe you can share with them that you once where not filled with joy until you discovered your own God-esteem. Whatever you do, do it in love, gentleness and kindness and remember, we are to uplift, heal and encourage.

Write Some of Your Thoughts:

What are your feelings about the joy within you? What is your understanding of your new God-esteem? How is it affecting your daily life and your view of yourself or if you are just getting started with this understanding, how do you think this will change your life?

_____

_____

_____

11

Keeping Safe As I Travel the Path

let us run with endurance the race that is set before us, looking unto Jesus, the author and finisher of our faith, who for the joy that was set before Him endured the cross[85]

What you have learned here and hopefully experienced along the way is the essence of faith. Faith is a shift from placing our belief in the world to placing our belief in Jesus Christ, that we can prosper while we journey in the world and have eternal life *NOW* and *FOREVER!* Remember the words of Jesus spoken to us at the beginning of chapter 4, "These things I have spoken to you, that My joy may remain in you, and that your joy may be full." The question for you at this point is, do you want your joy to be full?

In the Gospel of John we are told that Jesus came to the Pool of Bethesda and there He found a man who had an infirmity for 38 years, and the

---

[85] Hebrews 12:1b-2a

man was frustrated because he couldn't enter the pool where he felt he would be healed. He knew where he needed to be but didn't have the means to get there. When Jesus saw him He asked the infirmed and frustrated man, "Do you want to be made well?" The man knew his *need* but *the knowledge of our need is not enough, we must have a heartfelt want that will drive us in the right direction.* The want is our passion for what it is that will fill our need. "These things I have spoken to you that …your joy may be full." I left out the most important element of that statement by Jesus, "that My joy may remain in you". Your need is for joy and completion of perfect life, your want must be for Jesus who is the only One that can fulfill that need – that void within you. The fullness of our want is when we connect our need to the reality of the power of Jesus within us. The passion for Jesus grows out of one's known need. Once the passion is present in the heart of the believer then Jesus Himself will give assisting grace for that passion to be fulfilled – that is the realized present love of Jesus within – the fulfillment of joy – the reality of God-esteem!

The man at the pool was frustrated for the 38 years of his infirmity, because he didn't have the means to get into the pool. We also can experience frustration if we don't have the means to get into the presence of Jesus where we will be fulfilled, knowing joy and completeness. *Knowing our need and having a passion for Jesus is essential but there is more that is necessary for fulfillment and safety along the pathway of life.* Jesus understands this and provides us with the means of His grace for us to be assisted and directed in our healing process. Remember Jesus is present with you and is here to assist you and help you just as He did for that man at the Pool of Bethesda.

You may be familiar with these *means of grace* or these may be new to you, but either way, they are essential to our journey with Jesus and your continued process of healing and growth. *There is no substitute to God's means of grace in our faith journey. It will depend upon the strength of your longing, your degree of want in your heart.* That want in your heart will be your passion and that will determine whether or not you will find the joy Jesus is willing to full you with.

The man at the pool was reliant upon the world to get him into the water. He remained infirmed for 38 years because the powers of this world were insufficient. He knew his need and had the passion to endure but didn't have the means until Jesus intersected his path. This shows that the most significant form of the means of grace is the unity found in the gift of baptism. It is in the act of baptism that Jesus intersects each of us and takes us by the hand and leads us into the water of healing and restoration. It is in this act of baptism that, like that man at the pool, we release ourselves to the authority and power of Jesus and we do this in willful submission. In this way, the way of baptism, Jesus opens the door to the other forms of His assisting grace in our lives. [86]

Some of the means of grace are the reading of Scripture, the sharing and exploring of Scripture with others in small groups, the Lord's Supper, community worship, family and private prayer, fasting, taking time to listen to God, devotions, reflection, and meditation. It is essential to be with

---

[86] This is not to say that grace cannot be received until baptism is accomplished, no, not at all, but it does mean that the means of grace find their potential fulfillment through the realm of baptism.

fellow believers where you can guide and encourage each other, and yes, even at times with love, admonish each other. These means of grace are a blessing and are sweet to the human spirit when engaged with by faith. If you approach them as work or a task, then that is what they will be, however, if you approach them as a gift of God through Jesus Christ and the Holy Spirit then you will experience the joy of relationship of Jesus with you!

Another aspect of keeping you strong on you path of eternal life is the social connection. As the above means of grace strengthen your inward relationship with Christ Jesus and your heart grows and is filled with His love there is another transformation that will take place. Picture yourself in the likeness of the cross for a moment. The elongated vertical part is you, standing in the presence of Jesus as He showers His grace down upon you and through you. Your heart is touched, molded and filled to overflowing as you grow in the wonder of this grace. As a result you start to open up your arms, in love and acceptance to others. Wider and wider they open until there you stand in the mode of a living cross to the world – as a whole and living sacrifice of the love of Jesus for the world. In that process of your inward growth, your outward growth is matured and this in itself becomes another means of grace. So ministry and mission are two mature forms of grace for God's children. God has built this flow of grace on a *reciprocal principle*, the more that flows out, the greater is the amount that flows back and returns to the giver, eventually culminating in prayers of thanksgiving offerings to God – and the cycle is complete.

I encourage you to continue your shift into this new reality, into your God-esteem, your growth in the likeness of Jesus and your fulfillment of joy. If you are not in a faith community, find one where truth, love and grace abound. Pray and Jesus will guide you – He loves you more than His very own being. He has shown you this upon the Cross. If you are already in a faith community give yourself wholly to the process of growing into the likeness of Jesus Christ – with His love in your heart and His truth in your mind. With this I bid you the best in Christ Jesus. Remember the words that the angel Gabriel spoke to Mary, the mother of Jesus,

"For with God nothing will be impossible."[87] It is by faith that we grow into those words, live those words and have hope in those words. He has already uplifted your heart through this encounter with His truth and He will continue His work in you and you will find beautiful fulfillment of life – first in Him and then by Him that others may know this glory through you. Remember also, that as you go forward, life is a journey and that is the beautiful part. *We are on a journey of growth of closeness to Jesus and our journey is one of lifelong learning in and through Him.* What could be more exciting or beautiful – He is with you, He goes before you and He has in fact already made the way for you!

Let me close with this thought of encouragement from Thomas Kelly, a Christian from the Quaker family of our faith who lived in the early part of the 20th century. He himself was on a journey with Jesus and He wanted to draw closer to Jesus and give himself more wholly to Jesus –
and something wondrously beautiful happened. Jesus opened the flood gates of His love upon the heart and soul of Thomas. These words are an expression of what Jesus revealed to him and

---

[87] Luke 1:37.

something that all of us can experience. "The experience is of an invasion from beyond, of an Other who in gentle power breaks in upon our littleness and in tender expansiveness makes room for Himself. Had we thought Him an intruder? Nay, God's first odor is sweetness, God's touch an imparting of power. Suddenly, a tender giant walks by our side, no, strides within our puny footsteps. We are no longer our little selves. As two bodies closely fastened together and whirled in the air revolve in part about the heavier body, so life gets a new center, from which we are moved."[88]

May all of God's blessings be with you through Jesus Christ, the Son of God, and the Holy Spirit.

I bid you all love, peace and joy –

---

[88] Thomas Kelly, *The Sanctuary of the Soul* (Nashville: Upper Room Books), 25.

Reading List
For Continual Growing in Your Inner-strength

Making Life a Prayer: Selected Writings of John Cassian, Keith Beasley-Topliffe, ed., Nashville: Upper Room Books, 1997.

Streams of Living Water: Celebrating the Great Traditions of Christian Faith, Richard Foster, New York: HarperCollins, 1998.

Too Deep for Words: Rediscovering Lectio Divina, Thelma Hall, New York: Paulist Press, 1988.

Practicing the Presence of God, Brother Lawrence, Uhrichsville, Ohio: Barbour and Company, 1993.

Life of the Beloved: Spiritual Living in a Secular World, Henri J. M. Nouwen, New York:Crossroad Publishing, 1992.

The Only Necessary Thing: Living a Prayerful Life, Henri J. M. Nouwen, New York: Crossroad Publishing, 1999.

Communion with God, John Owen, R. F. K. Law, ed., Carlisle, PA: The Banner of Truth Trust, 1991.

Seeing Through the Eyes of Heaven: An Encounter with God, Gordon Van Namee, Mustang, OK: Tate Publishing, 2013.

Richard Peace has a series of books on spiritual development. Each covers a different area and acts as a building block for the other. They are interactive and instructional. They deal largely with the importance of the individual story.

Spiritual Journaling: Recording Your Journey Toward God, Richard Peace, Colorado Springs: Navpress, 1998.

The additional three books to this series are:
Spiritual Autobiography: Discovering and Sharing Your Spiritual Story
Contemplative Bible Reading: Experiencing God Through Scripture
Meditative Prayer: Entering God's Presence

Bibliography

Kelly, Thomas. *The Sanctuary of the Soul*. Nashville: Upper Room Books, 1997.

Kempis, Thomas a`. *The Imitation of Christ*. Translated by Aloysius Croft and Harold Bolton. Mineloa, New York: Dover Publications, 2003.

Rotelle, John E., ed. *Tradition Day by Day: Readings from Church Writers*. Villanova, PA: Augustinian Press, 1994.

Stein, Sol. *Stein on Writing*. New York: St. Martin's Press, 1995.

Wikipedia. Albert Pujols, en.wikipedia.org/wiki/Pojols (accessed March 24, 2014).

www.ingramcontent.com/pod-product-compliance
Lightning Source LLC
Chambersburg PA
CBHW070800100426
42742CB00012B/2208